RAIDER

RAIDER

THE RAYMOND CHESTER STORY

JON GOWER

Calon

2025

www.uwp.co.uk

British Library Cataloguing-in-Publication Data
A catalogue record for this book is available from the British Library.

ISBN: 978-1-915279-94-1

For GPSR enquiries please contact: Easy Access System Europe Oü, 16879218. Mustam.e tee 50, 10621, Tallinn, Estonia. gpsr.requests@easproject.com

Cover image by Focus on Sport/Getty Images
Cover design by Andy Ward
Typeset by Agnes Graves
Printed and bound in Great Britain by Bell & Bain Ltd, Glasgow

'Wherever you go, you are the Oakland Raiders...
I don't care who you are or what you've done.
You're here now, and you're going to win, win, win.'
(*Al Davis*)

'Seven days a week, it was as much fun
as a human being could have and still stay alive.'
(*Bob Moore*)

CONTENTS

AUTHOR'S PREFACE

I well remember the first time I met Raymond Chester. My wife Sarah and I were celebrating an upgrade on our room in a San Francisco hotel, as it meant we had more room to hide chocolate eggs for our daughters to hunt down. We'd promised them that the Easter Bunny wouldn't forget about them just because they were 4,500 miles away from home in Cardiff, Wales.

Sarah comes from Oakland, California, so every trip to the West Coast involved family visits. On this particular occasion, we were going to be meeting one of her sisters, Martha, along with her partner Raymond. He, Raymond Chester, turned out to be an utterly charming man – open, engaging and a born storyteller, although I also recall that shaking hands with him actually hurt. It suggested he might sometimes forget the difference between a person's grip and clamping down on a pair of dumbbells. Or at least that's what it felt like. Now in his seventies, here was a man of great physical strength, and he still diligently worked out in the gym and cycled for fun over the Bay Bridge between Oakland and San Francisco, showing his physical mettle. Somewhere in the conversation, he mentioned he'd been a footballer. To me, this meant what we call *American* football, which conjured up images of human wrecking balls smashing into each other at speed. It was hard to reconcile this with the gentle man in front of me, smiling broadly as he shared his stories.

I've always been fascinated by American culture, reading my way through the work of the literary heavyweights with great delight. I have been lucky enough to interview some of them, luminaries such as Richard Ford and Gore Vidal; the latter teasingly suggested that he had family roots in Wales and that his first name was a corruption of my surname, Gower thus becoming Gore. And then I had the great good fortune to spend a day with the one literary hero whose work I had read in its entirety, John Updike, who turned out to be what all such heroes should be, namely, gracious to a fault.

And of course there was the music, spanning from Springsteen to Kendrick Lamar, not forgetting the perfect pop singles of Motown or one of my all-time favourites, The Doobie Brothers. So, despite growing up in Wales, part of my head was always in the States, delighting in its diversity and its energy. I then married a Californian and the connection duly deepened.

Convivially chatting with Raymond was initially a bit like the time I spent with Updike, even though what I knew about the NFL (National Football League) and what we call American football on our side of the pond could be written down on the back of a postage stamp. A small postage stamp at that. One you'd look at under a microscope to make out the detail. I'm a rugby fan, one who reasonably expects to have a heart attack at the exact moment Wales scores a try against the old, old enemy England. But when Raymond started telling me about the length of his career, outlined his philosophy and started to recall certain key moments in both his playing and personal history, this diehard, lifelong rugby fan found himself completely enthralled, just as I was in the company of the great John Updike.

Raymond had me transfixed as he told me about the 1968 game between Morgan State and Grambling, two Black historical colleges who found themselves facing off at a time when America was convulsed after the assassination of Dr Martin Luther King. With riots on the streets and some cities literally in flames, there were many who didn't want the game to go ahead, citing the racial tension across the United States as reason enough to cancel.

Raymond recalled the importance of the match-up between Morgan State and Grambling, having no doubt whatsoever about what it represented.

It was probably the most significant game of my life, from a lot of standpoints. If you set the scene for it, it was Martin Luther King, it was Bobby Kennedy, it was John Kennedy a few years before that. The game was scheduled at Yankee Stadium, and it was the first time in history that two Black historical colleges were going to play at that stadium, on that size stage. And they were expecting seventy or seventy-five thousand people in the stands. Then, lo and behold, Martin Luther King gets assassinated and then they were thinking about canceling the game because the whole country was in chaos, just chaos.

But the clash did go ahead, and Raymond duly scored all the points as Morgan State came out the winners. More importantly, it was a pivotal game because it led to the NFL paying more attention to Black players and starting to recruit them. You could say the game helped change the colour of the participants amid the convulsions of the civil rights movement: it was that important.

So I started to do some basic research about the game. Some very, very basic research to begin with. I bought *American Football for Dummies* and read it twice because I didn't fully understand it the first time round. But that said, and in my defence, rugby can be utterly perplexing for an NFL fan. I watched lots of footage of games, not least a sequence which showed Raymond shrugging off would-be tacklers as if they were wraiths. I thought this was an exquisite display of that selfsame strength I felt the first time Raymond shook my hand, but he suggested otherwise, that what was on display in that game was a fine sense of balance. Looking at it again, and with that corrective, made me appreciate the skills on show even more. Not running, but dancing.

It soon became apparent that here was a story waiting to be told, one which embraced supreme athleticism, top-level team-playing and a personal, unwavering dedication to the requirements of a sport. It was also a tale of longevity as here was a player who had a very long career, a slow, steady burn as opposed to the firework bursts of so many players. The average career of an NFL player spans 3.3 years, and even those can take a physical toll. In Raymond's case he played for some thirteen years, with the final one as part of a newbie league, the United States Football League (USFL), set up to challenge the mighty NFL itself. The fledgling league didn't last, but Raymond certainly did.

Raymond and I got on famously. So when I broached the subject of writing a book about his life, he paid me the courtesy of not laughing out loud.

Rather, we started a series of interviews and conversations, which happened in a range of excellent locations, from my favourite pub in Wales, the Murenger in Newport, to a great bar in Oakland, sadly now defunct, namely Luka's Taproom and Grill. In between, there were some long and absorbing conversations at the bar of the Lake Chabot Golf Club, the convivial hostelry that is the Three Tuns in Chepstow and the Beverley pub in Cardiff, as well as various visits to enjoy sushi or savour perfectly mixed margaritas in Californian cocktail bars and cantinas. I know there's the danger that listing these locations one after the other makes it sound as if we should both presently be checking into rehab, but spending time with Raymond felt like a holiday and, truth be told, writing this book often didn't feel like work. More a pleasure and privilege. Lots and lots of champagne moments. Because writing it helped cement a feeling of friendship and an unlikely one at that. Hours of 'research' were in truth full of entertainment and laughter. Imagine the rugby-loving son of a railwayman and a shop assistant from a coal mining community in south Wales hanging out with a Super Bowl winner and having the temerity to even use the term 'tight end' let alone pontificate on it a little, or, later on, to even *start* to analyse games in his company. But friendship it is, and love and respect are its twin cements.

Raymond with the author (Photo: Martha Hill)

What emerged from all the conversations and interviews is the tale of a man born with natural sporting ability, but also one blessed with the good sense of knowing that these could always be improved, to be taken one level higher. It was also a life story where a challenging childhood was never left behind entirely, as those memories and shaping experiences helped fashion the man Raymond became. Remembering where you come from often helps you steer a clear path through life's thickets.

Raider is the story of how a man is shaped and shapes himself, indeed of how he gets into shape and finds the moral fulcrum on which to turn, which in turn gives him strength. It's also the tale of a man who rails against some of the injustice in the world in a pragmatic way, by the simple act of helping others. And always plays in and for the team. Always the team.

Sport, like music, is a universal language which speaks to us all about how we can be better, work harder and set out personal goals of achievement, range and purpose. It doesn't matter if you're a football fan, a rugby supporter, a player of tennis or an observer of golf, the qualities of the best players, the heroines and heroes of the game, are easily agreed upon. They are diligence, practice, discipline, application and bloody hard work, to mention just a few. And like art, sport holds up a mirror to society, to its blemishes and its beauty. In portraying one of the NFL's longest-serving players, Raymond Chester, this book also looks at some of the societal changes that were happening all around him. He is an extraordinary man who trained and played with other extraordinary athletes, running over fields of glory towards the touchdown, putting in the hard yards, running routes around the opponents and ideally leaving them standing.

For perhaps, more than anything else, *Raider* is the story of solidly being *a team player*, of being one musician in a band of brothers, who played their own mad tune on the football field, a brazen and brilliant marching band call to action which required perfect timing, intuition and togetherness. Blast out the horns! Encourage the roar of the spectators' voices! Playing the Raider way, which really could be a symphony in motion, something beautiful and exhilarating to watch, where a deft pass could sound a duff note or allow a fellow player to be fully on song and push for the line. Where putting all the notes together on the playing field made a raucous, physical music more marvellous, loud, transfixing and yet controlled that could rival all the bellowing hooting and hollering yells of the travelling ultra-vocal army of Raider fans. Yes, a music that loud and glorious and symphonic and true. And then some.

FOREWORD:

A BAND OF BROTHERS
BY RAYMOND CHESTER

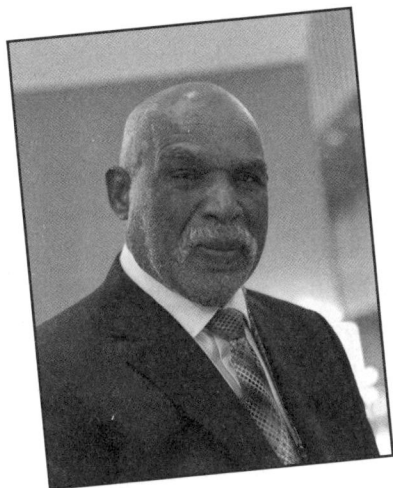

Raymond today (Photo: Martha Hill)

In a team like the Raiders, you struggle together, you grow together, you achieve together and you fail together. When you take the time, over time, to get to know each other, you eventually get to know the soul of a man. Some guys will not be honest, not be true, not make the full commitment, but sooner or later they will fall by the wayside. But then you have the Lamonicas and the Blandas; they're players that I loved and they loved me. If you're new to my story, don't worry; this book will introduce them and my other teammates to you. Every one an athlete. Every one a special individual, but always a member of the team, fully committed to working as a unit, working together to win. One of the principal reasons we played so well together was because we didn't want to let each other down. I was committed to them; they were committed to me.

And what was my commitment exactly? To do my job, do the best job that I could possibly do and contribute in every way I legally could to achieve the goal of the team. We worked hard to get better. Don't cheapen that by saying we cheated to win or we were dirty. We played hard. There was a rule in practice, and on the field, that said the first one who cries is a sissy, so don't cry about being hit hard or getting beaten down or worn out or being made to quit. Don't cry about that, because that's the game; that's the way the game is.

In my life – a life that has had the good, the bad and the ugly – the thing that was paramount was love. Growing up, I had loving, God-fearing parents, and there was an emphasis on education, on respect and on love, and right to this day, we're still a close family. All the folks in my family – my brothers, my sisters, my children and, in turn, their children – love each other.

That bond is true for fellow players as well as for family. The Raiders won because we were a band of brothers. We loved each other despite some of the stupid stuff we did and the mistakes we made. *We were a team.* Now you have to give credit to coaches and managers such as John Madden, Tom Flores and Al Davis for allowing us to be that, to take individuals from all over America and turn them into a team. It wasn't like they were training lions, where they would have five animals in a cage, throw in enough meat for three and watch them fight it out. When people try to portray the Raiders that way, it just burns me up. Because when I talk on the phone to, say, former tight end Ron Wheeler, the last thing we say is 'Love you, man'.

People are always in search of the key, the Holy Grail: asking how did a team such as the Raiders win and win? How can a team do that today? What's the driving force of success? It's simple. *I don't want to let my brother down.*

The Raiders were as good as we were because we worked harder and we practised longer than any other team in the league. We stayed after practice. We talked about the game and considered how we played, one player conferring with the next even though we might actually be in competition for the same position. Take Dave Casper, for instance, a fellow tight end on the Raiders team with me. He was nicknamed 'The Ghost' after the cartoon character Casper the Friendly Ghost, not that players who faced him would have thought he was all that friendly or ghostly if he crunched into them. The competition between the two of us was legendary, just as our accomplishments are unbelievable. Here we had two players in the same position on the same team make the All-Star team, make All-Pro in the same year. It's crazy. The reason we did that and were able to do that was the ethic we had with regard to practice and the way we felt about trying to help each other to do their job and be the best they could be. Everybody nowadays, on TV and so on, purports to know what's wrong with such and such a team, but what I'm going to say is the players don't have enough love for each other.

That's the attitude we displayed, that we personified. It makes me so angry when they talk about the Raiders partying and drinking and breaking the law. The reason we won and kept on winning was that we were in better shape; we were the best-conditioned team in the league. We stayed in training camp for seven weeks. Do you know how long they stay in training camp now? Ten days! They want to say we were always drunk and partying: are you kidding me? How did we win so many games in the waning moments, in the fourth quarter? Why is that? Because we were drunk and out of shape? I don't think so.

If you look at many sports, what truly matters is the essence of teamwork, building camaraderie and championship teams and building the respect you need to be successful in sport. In pro-sport, you have situations where people buy in the best players and so achieve temporary success, but it simply won't last unless you've got the chemistry, you have the necessary culture and you know where to put the emphasis in that culture. If you don't have the work ethic and the commitment, it isn't possible to win, and to win over and over again as we did.

Here were gifted, dedicated men from whom I and many others could draw strength and confidence: Cliff Branch, Henry Lawrence and Morris Bradshaw were my roommates! Kenny Stabler and Jim Plunkett were both great leaders and super QBs. The roster of superb fellow players includes Jack Tatum, Clarence Davis and Charlie Smith; athletes Derrick Ramsey and Willie Brown; great Raiders such as Bob Chandler, Dave Dalby, George Atkinson and Dave Casper; alongside courageous footballer players such as Ray Guy, Jim Otto, Rod Martin, Bob Brown and Art Shell. I am grateful also to warriors such as Kenny King, Otis Sistrunk, Gene Upshaw, Ted Hendricks and so many more truly outstanding players that to this day, I am proud to call brothers and friends. They were all so relevant in the development of said winning culture!

'One for all and all for one.'

The Raiders of the 1970s and 1980s were classic examples of that phrase, that motto. We live its truth even to this day.

People sometimes think we won because we had the best players, the biggest players, the biggest names, the fastest, the strongest athletes, but the truth of the matter is that maybe that works for you one or two times, but it will not sustain itself, not without having key ingredients such as fellowship and unselfishness. Much of the time, teams do well, and there are guys who get all of the publicity and make all the money, but they could never make it without guys who allow them to step on their backs. That's how I always saw myself: I was one of those players. I didn't need to be up there, to get rewards and awards. I was the sort of guy you could depend on – yes, you can step on my back to get up there. And we had a bunch of such guys on the team. They made a solid foundation.

I still keep in touch with many old players, though many are no longer with us. We may have an email exchange or a text feed with seven or eight guys involved all over the country. Nine times out of ten, the conversation ends with 'Take care of yourself, I love you, bro.' *I love you.* That love was displayed both on the field and in practice. You can't cheapen or dismiss the power of that kind of interaction or affection for each other – of genuine respect and love for each other. Love is the missing component, that and dependability. Love is one of the most powerful things, so you have to put that power to use, put it to work. Love is commitment; love is protection, sacrifice and sharing. Love is courageous and it may sound silly when you're talking about a competitive sport such as football but, when you win a championship, love will help you execute that. As it did for us. Over and over again.

Raymond Chester
Oakland, California, January 2024

PART ONE:

GAME-CHANGER 1968

1.

THE GRAMBLING VERSUS MORGAN INVITATIONAL FOOTBALL CLASSIC

That afternoon at Yankee Stadium conjured up memories of Negro League baseball games of the 1940s and Harlem Rens basketball games at the Renaissance Ballroom.

This was a snapshot of our past, our present, and – I hoped – our future.

I walked off the Yankee Stadium turf bursting with pride, thankful to be part of something this big, this black, this beautiful. We had the athletes, the fans, had the money. This day, I thought, was the beginning of something. After all that had happened in 1968 – the assassinations, the riots, the protests – things would never be the same again; there was no going back.

(William C. Rhoden, *Forty Million Dollar Slaves: The Rise, Fall and Redemption of the Black Athlete*)

Very few football games change history. This one did. On September 28, 1968, two Black historical colleges lined up against each other for the first time. Two very different animals, too. Louisiana's Grambling College Tigers faced Baltimore's Morgan State Bears, who were arriving with an undefeated record they were determined to defend just as eagerly as the Tigers wanted to claw it away. To add to the immense sense of occasion, they were clashing in a world-famous venue, in Yankee Stadium, that iconic New York temple to sport. History *was* in the making.

The game made the authorities jittery, to say the least. Civil unrest was edging towards the pandemic. American cities were in flames. The idea of sixty thousand Black fans, possibly more, gathering in one location in the Bronx set minds racing with images of police in riot gear, batons in hand, of cars and buildings set ablaze as volatile anger in the air mixed with the sting of tear gas.

Much of that tumultuous year of 1968 had been riven by protests and spreading racial discontent, and the game was due to take place a mere five months after Martin Luther King's assassination. In the wake of that killing in Memphis, there had been riots all over America: in Boston, New York, Newark, Trenton, Baltimore, Pittsburgh, Cincinnati, Detroit, Chicago, Nashville, Kansas City and Oakland, and of course in Memphis itself, as well as more than a hundred smaller cities and towns. In early April, President Lyndon Johnson was forced to call out thousands of federal troops to quell riots on the streets of Washington itself, and before quiet was restored, over fifty thousand members of the Army and National Guard were on riot duty. This was the backdrop to the game. Oil needed to be poured on troubled water. As Robert Kennedy put it, speaking after the assassination of Dr King:

> For those of you who are Black – considering the evidence there evidently is that there were white people who were responsible – you can be filled with bitterness, with hatred and a desire for revenge. We can move in that direction as a country, in great polarization – Black people among Black, white people amongst white, filled with hatred toward one another.

Or we can make an effort, as Martin Luther King did, to understand and to comprehend, and to replace that violence, that stain of bloodshed that has spread across our land, with an effort to understand with compassion and love.[1]

Now football fans usually get worked up: fervid rivalry is part of the sporting drama. But there was far too much tension in the air already. Civil rights were being asserted right across America. Cities were being put to the torch.

Howard Berk was the Yankees' vice president in charge of administration at the time. He knew that people such as city officials, the police department and senior CBS management were concerned about the volatile situation. Berk duly had to get a letter from City Hall saying that the city would provide extra security due to the presence of so many Black people and the concern about the possibility of some kind of violence, of there being riots.

The players too had picked up on the troubled vibe. Former Morgan State running back George Nock had heard that the powers that be were really afraid of Black people coming together and what would transpire after that. The newspapers, stadium officials and the civic authorities all twitched out nervous messages about what might go wrong. This could be a *game* or this could be a *tragedy*, as the hysterical hype had it.

Morgan State tight end Raymond Chester (hereafter just called Raymond, as one does with friends) remembers both the profound sense of occasion and the sheer, simple significance of that September day.

> What I remember is how important it was and then as all the events began to unfold – the death, the assassination of Martin Luther King, and all the civil rights issues that were swirling around, especially after Robert Kennedy had just given that famous speech after Doctor King's death – it was crazy. Then here we go to New York, and we're inviting all of these kids and their fans from Grambling and Morgan

State. They had meetings, they talked about canceling the game, they talked about what the potential was for problems, for riots. But what they underestimated was the tremendous leadership qualities of both of those coaches, the coach for Grambling named Eddie Robinson and the coach for Morgan – Earl Banks – and the tremendous influence those guys had, not only on the teams but on the entire colleges and on their entire conferences and indeed on the entire foundation of the Black historical colleges. Those two guys were the most influential historical Black college leaders in the country. And they used that influence and their magic over not just their teams but over their fans and over their administrators. And they made it obvious how important it was that we pull this thing off and nobody should screw it up.[2]

Earl Banks was an inspiring coach who left an indelible mark on Raymond, not least with the somewhat surprising way he employed silence as a tool.

Before our big games, we would go out onto the field to start warming up at our end while the other team was down the other. Guess what our MO was at Morgan when we went on the field? You won't believe this. Our players didn't say a word. There was nothing. We'd warm up, and all you'd hear was pads. The coaches would tell us where we had to go and how to stretch, and we would do these group calisthenics, but you wouldn't hear a word from the senior players. And that was our motto; that was our thing at Morgan. You don't talk shit: you knock the shit out of them. And that's what we did.

If you faced Morgan, you didn't hear anything – just the guys doing their exercise and running their drills. But if you know anything about it, that's deafening. That's scary as shit. It says these guys are for real.

Morgan State found success in other sports too. It developed a lacrosse team for which 'Chip' Silverman recruited a handful of football players, mostly second-team guys, not the stars. The team was formed in 1970 when a former Baltimore high school lacrosse player and Morgan grad student, Howard 'Chip' Silverman, realised that many of Baltimore's Black high school lacrosse players were at Morgan but were not playing lacrosse. Silverman had never coached before, but he put up flyers around campus, and thirty athletes showed up for a meeting. Two-thirds were football players. Some would later star in the NFL, such as Stan Cherry. Silverman started the lacrosse club and two years later petitioned the NCAA (National Collegiate Athletic Association) for full membership as a college team. At that time, the NCAA had its best forty teams in Division I and another eighty teams in Division II. It was Division II that Morgan would soon dominate. The lacrosse team performed so well that they challenged Navy, John Hopkins and some of the other big schools.

Back to football. Come the day of the big game, the crowds flowed towards Yankee Stadium on foot, by bus and on the subway, pouring in from the city's boroughs and from adjoining states, not to mention the legion of college fans who had travelled from Maryland and Louisiana to support the two teams.

They were all converging on a great sporting amphitheatre that looked as if it was carved out of a single piece of limestone and shaped like a huge round of cheese. Had anyone asked, they might have found out that it was actually built using a special kind of super-concrete, patented by Thomas Edison, the king of US inventors. But this was to be a day about sport, not science. They were here to celebrate a national game and display of human excellence and exceptionalism as it is manifested on the sports field. Athleticism. Power. Running, and running hard. Hitting, hitting hard, bone on bone, crunching body to body. Thinking on one's feet. Making the hard yards. Playing as a team while shining as an individual. Taking orders or cutting loose. Crashing into contact with a huge man coming the other way. At speed. The excitement everywhere was palpable.

But *there was science* to the day. Coaching football is both an art and a science, and in Morgan State's case, the coach actually *was* a scientist. Earl Banks had been educated in the public schools of Chicago, had graduated from Wendell Phillips High School and held a Bachelor of Science degree from the University of Iowa as well as a Master of Science degree from New York University. He had also won his spurs as a player, with four years under his belt of 'Big Ten' football at the University of Iowa, not to mention one year's professional experience with the New York Yankees in the Old American Football League. He was no slouch when it came to coaching either. Banks, this former All-American and member of the All-America Conference, had been head coach of Morgan State since 1960, guiding them to four Central Intercollegiate Athletic Association (CIAA) championships and a record of 55-11-1.

Morgan's Earl Banks, along with Eddie Robinson from Grambling, had attended Martin Luther King's funeral in King's Ebenezer Baptist Church in Atlanta in April, where they also met Florida A & M coach Jake Gaither. They sweltered along with the rest of the congregation and watched the coffin on an old green farm wagon being pulled by two mules through the city streets, en route for another memorial service for Dr King at Morehouse College.

Meanwhile, Grambling PR guru Collie J. Nicholson had put on his best tie and gone to Madison Avenue in Manhattan to look for sponsorship. It wasn't an easy pitch for a small school from Louisiana, but he struck lucky in the offices of Ballantine beer, who joined with the Football Managers Federation in ensuring that every dollar of profit from the proposed game would go to the NY Urban League. This was an organisation which would, in the words of one of the adverts for the game, 'Help give a dropout a fresh start toward a good education.' Why did the beer money flow? Ballantine had been in its own battle, against its rival Rheingold, and saw sponsoring the game as a way of getting a bigger slice of a lucrative market filled with Black consumers.

There were dimensions other than commercial ones, of course. Grambling coach Eddie Robinson had long been troubled by the problems of Black education in America. He had been in touch with the Urban League of Greater New York, headquartered on West 136th Street, in the heart of Harlem, to try to find a way to use football to help. It was proposed that the game would raise money for underprivileged urban youth who were trying to gain a toehold on the first rung of the educational ladder. This would mainly happen through the street academy programmes, which allowed them to study for a degree outside of a conventional higher educational setting. The academies were often found in stores, so a young person could just walk right in off the street. In Harlem, school dropout rates were running off the graph. Couple that with civil rights protests, fomenting an area riddled with crime and blighted by housing problems – not to mention the gnawing urges of poverty and hunger – and you had a powder keg situation set to blow up. One football game couldn't solve all of those problems, but it could make a start.

The weekend after MLK's funeral, three coaches – Robinson, Banks and Jake Gaither from Florida A & M University – met with Ballantine beer executive Bill Curtis, manager of market development for the firm, to finalise a deal for the benefit game at Yankee Stadium, in the same breath setting up the Football Managers' Federation.

They had to choose which of the three teams would play. Gaither decided to back out, leaving Grambling to play Morgan State, thereby leaving two top coaches and their respective teams against each other.

Eddie Gay Robinson had started his exceptional career as Grambling head coach in 1941 and had been cited by the Football Writers' Association in Chicago as the man who made the greatest contribution to small college football during the last twenty-five years.

Here was a man who'd had an interesting life. Samuel G. Freedman encapsulates the early years in his book *Breaking the Line*. Saying Robinson was the only child of 'a third generation sharecropper and a maid who earned a dollar a day. He had spent his first six years in the farming town of Jackson, south Louisiana, sleeping on the floor of a shotgun shack without heat, water or electricity, connected by a plankway to the outhouse.'³ After his parents divorced, the young man moved with his dad to a segregated neighbourhood in Baton Rouge, namely South Baton Rouge, where he 'shined shoes, hawked papers, hauled ice, cut hair, bused tables, bagged shrimp, sold strawberries, delivered sandwiches' and also learned how to box, which allowed him to walk the streets with the gloves draped over his shoulders. This was the man who grew up to coach Grambling for one of the biggest games in the college's history, taking on Morgan State.

Morgan State University in Baltimore, Maryland, had been founded two years after the Civil War and had a rich football tradition. There, coach Eddie Hurt had enjoyed six undefeated seasons, and at one time Morgan State had a stretch of no fewer than forty-two wins, no losses and six ties. In the 1930s and 1940s, Morgan State was certainly a major player in Black college football.

When Earl Banks came along, he had his work cut out for him, having to follow a class act in the form of Eddie Hurt. But Banks soon made his mark, not least by getting players into the pros. Morgan State linebacker Willie Lanier, for instance, was one of three Morgan State players drafted by the NFL in 1976. He told a CBS interviewer that 'Banks was building a programme that would not only have the ability to compete at a college level but for those few players who had the skills to go further he was really trying to build a standard, and that standard was both academic and athletic combined and he was focussed on that completely.'⁴

Raymond was the Morgan State tight end between 1966 and 1969 and remembers Banks vividly: 'Very talented, he was a gifted orator, he was a strategist, he was a motivator, he was a disciplinarian, he was just a man for all seasons.' Similarly, George Nock, a Morgan State running back between 1964 and 1968, maintained that Banks 'instilled in us the will to win, the will to overcome against any odds'.⁵

For many people, knowledge of Black college football, indeed of its very existence, brought with it the shock of the new. The changes wrought by emancipation included a fierce desire for education on the part of former slaves. That need to learn to read and write was met by the Black colleges that helped teach an entire generation. The early colleges sprouted up in churches, open fields and abandoned barns, anywhere a class could be held. As the thirst for education grew, so too did historically Black colleges and universities.

A Black football game was a real spectacle, with the fans often putting in a high-octane performance matched by extravagant marching bands that managed to mix regimented discipline with near-religious fervour. Batons twirled as cheerleaders high-kicked. A game was part picnic for a hugely extended family, part church meeting, part R & B concert and somewhere among the songs and cheerleading razzmatazz, they played a bit of football. And played it with plenty of skill, a deep seriousness of focus and game-planning strategy, which was all often widely overlooked.

That day in September 1968, 'We had something to prove,'[6] suggested Mark Washington, who started as a freshman defensive back for Morgan State and subsequently played for ten years in the NFL. The Bears had been the first to integrate the Tangerine Bowl in Orlando, defeating the West Chester (Pennsylvania) Rams in 1966. In 1967 they were again undefeated and ranked in the national Top 10 by the Associated Press. But they weren't invited back to a bowl game.

Washington wasn't alone in feeling that they had been neglected, and not just by white audiences. All of Black America, all of the Black colleges, would be looking at this game as a major event and as that rarest of opportunities, a game to break barriers down if not smash them. Black college football had been around a long time, but it had never had a showcase anything like this.

Eddie Robinson at Grambling had been doing his determined best to break those selfsame barriers in a former agricultural college. Between the 1940s and 1980s, Grambling became nothing less than a football factory. Robinson, a one-man show when it came to coaching, was often described as a genius, displaying rare skills even as early as his second year when he had an undefeated season at the helm. Robinson wanted nothing less than for Grambling to be the Black Notre Dame. He wanted Black players to have the same opportunities as white. Race was ever a consideration.

One of Robinson's other driving ambitions was to send a Black player into what was then an almost completely white NFL. He needed a tank to break through the colour barrier and found one in the shape of Paul 'Tank' Younger, a man one could fairly describe as the Jackie Robinson of football. He had been given the nickname by the visionary PR man Collie J. Nicholson, who worked for Grambling as sports information director for three decades. Nicholson invented monikers for all the players and drove all over the state making sure local newspapers carried stories about his college team.

Helpfully, Grambling had gained a certain prominence in Black football courtesy of a TV documentary. The veteran sportswriter Jerry Izenberg had written an article about Grambling for *True* magazine, which in turn led to a TV documentary being made by him and producer Howard Cosell called *Grambling College: 100 Yards to Glory*. The arc lamp of publicity had never been trained on Black college football up to this point. And TV was in the very active process of growing a huge audience, so a moment in the limelight could have a great deal of influence. As this moment most certainly did.

One of the people who saw the documentary was New York Yankees' president E. Michael Burke, who duly phoned Izenberg and asked why they didn't put the team on in Yankee Stadium. The Yankees' VP of administration, Howard Berk, a native New Yorker and Marine Corps veteran, felt that the Yankees had been very remiss in not supporting the African-American market, and this brought everybody into one place. Grambling College also saw this as a great opportunity, even though there were many detractors who doubted that Black college football could fill such a huge stadium. And the coaches brought plenty of enthusiasm. O.K. Davis, of the *Ruston Daily Leader*, suggests that Banks was perhaps the East Coast equivalent to Eddie Robinson, the type of person who had a very big impact on young people.

Morgan State could almost match Grambling's productivity rate when it came to producing professional players such as NFL Hall of Famers Roosevelt Brown, Leroy Kelly and Willie Lanier. Two teams with two powerful histories were set to play ball. Raymond well recalls how 'everybody knew about the great Eddie Robinson and all the great players that had come from Grambling.'

But on the other hand, Morgan State were no slouches. In 1968 they had won twenty-six consecutive games heading into New York and featured future Super Bowl champion running back John 'Frenchy' Fuqua as well as players of the unquestionable calibre of Raymond Chester. Meanwhile, the Grambling Tigers were led on field by another of coach Robinson's barrier-breakers, the quarterback James 'Shack' Harris, who was set to become the NFL's first successful Black quarterback. Grambling knew the calibre of players they had on the football team but also recognised the challenge ahead. Here were two teams that came from winning traditions, two teams that most certainly didn't want to lose. But sport, being a somewhat cruel endeavour, means one team wins, while one is vanquished.

2.

THE BIG DAY APPROACHES

Both teams arrived in New York City on the Friday, one day before the game was due to take place. It was Morgan State's opening game of the season and for Grambling the second. Here were two teams that fair matched each other in the battle of successes, with Morgan State unbeaten for a run of no fewer than twenty-six games, stretching back to the fourth game of the season in 1964.

Grambling, meanwhile, was the defending Black national champion, so there was everything and more to play for. The two teams hadn't faced each other since 1945, when the then-president of Grambling, Ralph Waldo Emerson Jones, was busily trying to turn it into the equivalent to Notre Dame when it came to Black college football. The plan certainly didn't deliver that year, when Grambling was completely and utterly trounced, 0–35. Undeterred, Grambling stuck to its ambitious path, and by September 1968, it had more players on the professional rosters than any college other than Notre Dame. So putting the two teams up against each other was much more than a competition between strength, skill and strategy. As William C. Rhoden put it, this was much bigger than a game. It was an illustration 'of the power of the African-American college, the power of the African-American consumer, and the power of the African-American athletes at the historically Black institution'.[7]

For some of the players it wasn't just a visit out of state, for some it was a trip out of this world. The USA's biggest city was a simply overwhelming sight for players from small-town America. Doug Porter had to convince quite a few of the players to even accept flying there in the first place. Many of the Grambling guys had never flown before, so it was a daunting prospect. Some players hadn't ventured out of the great state of Louisiana in their entire lives. James 'Shack' Harris, the Grambling quarterback from 1965 to 1968, recalled that many of his fellow players hadn't been on a plane before, so a couple of guys on the plane tried to open a window to get some air.

They were given a tour of the Big Apple on the way to the hotel. Grambling cornerback Delles Howell recalled seeing some sights and things going on in New York that just blew their minds. The same was true for Morgan State as they took in the city sounds and spectacles. Raymond's memory of Morgan State's tour around the Big Apple literally snakes into his mind: 'We saw a guy walking down the street with a python around his neck. I'll never forget that, a big python snake around his neck. Man, we all just crowded around to the bus window and guys ran over to see it. You saw all kinds of things: it was like going to Disneyland.'

A combination of big city and pre-game nerves set off nervous butterflies. Even the hotel architecture could flummox. Grambling's 'Shack' Harris recalled how they had one guy who missed a meeting because he wasn't going to walk back down all the stairs from his room: he didn't know they had an elevator. The players saw guys who had a dice game going on right round the corner from where some police were sitting. For some of the country boys, the sights, sounds and sheer spectacle of the city were close to overwhelming.

Even Eddie Robinson, who was a well-travelled man – both Stateside and overseas – had never been to Harlem, and with tension simmering all across America, this wasn't necessarily a good time to be visiting its hoods. As the team was driving through the neighbourhood, players from places such as Jonesboro, Arkansas and Bernice, Louisiana, took in the scenes, the vistas of desperate streets and unemployed guys just hanging around. Robinson saw this as a life lesson, telling his players that if they had college diplomas, they were never going to be one of those standing around on any street corner.

But the street scenes, despite the visible poverty, were also ablaze with colour, energy and character, as William C. Rhoden recalled. The veteran sportswriter was one of four freshmen in the Morgan State squad, although he didn't play in the game itself. He noted how spirits were soaring at the end of another hard week in Harlem, one 'great, busy drama of huge Afros and processed hair…Red, black and green liberation flags flew everywhere…

'Cool cats sported canary yellow suits, while Superfly brothers in shades leaned against shining Eldorados with gangster whitewalls.'[8]

Coach Banks, who had studied at New York University, where he had gained his master's degree as well as playing professional football for the New York Yankees in the All-America Football Conference, transformed into the local tour guide, showing his players the roster of hit spots, such as the Showman's Lounge, the Red Rooster and the Hotel Theresa. He gave them both colour and detail, such as informing his wide-eyed party that you could always tell the prostitutes by the white boots they wore.

Pressure on the players had of course been building long before they left home to travel to New York. Raymond recalls:

> At the same time that you would have thought that that kind of pressure would have had a negative effect on the young guys like us, but we had a solution to that, and that was practice, work hard and practice more to understand what we had to do and have confidence. And we had built that confidence for seasons, losing only four games in four years. So we had a great team, and Grambling had one too. And they had a whole list of great players who were in the pros, in basketball, football.

It was a time for some cool and concentrated football thinking. The Morgan State Bears approached the game 'as if we should have been playing nationally a long time ago', according to running back George Nock. 'I couldn't understand why our universities didn't get together and have a national playoff in which championship winning teams such as Grambling, Morgan State, Tennessee and Florida A & M pooled resources' and thus shared the limelight, knowing, as Nock put it, that 'much of the HBCUs [historically Black colleges] had the best of the best'.[9]

Raymond recalls how the febrile atmosphere of the day built up hour by hour, minute by minute.

I can remember the pressure leading up to that game. First of all, Morgan was a phenomenal school in terms of its athletic record. We thought we could beat any school – we could beat USC, we could beat Notre Dame and Texas – we would have played anyone, because we thought our team was just that great. And there were a lot of people who thought so too.

Of course, those schools would never play us because they had everything to lose reputation-wise and nothing whatsoever to gain. So we had had this phenomenal win-streak and record in our division. Grambling had an equal reputation, if not better. And so, to try to bring those teams together, they were trying to promote historical Black college football and Black athletes. Now they didn't have to go too far to promote it because Black athletes were coming out of these small colleges, and they were permeating the NFL, the NBA and the professional leagues at a tremendous ratio for the size of the schools and the number of schools and the number of players. But the universities were looking for a way to take advantage of this and they were coming in and harvesting all our young players, and they were making money and playing great for the NFL. How do we harvest that?

17

When the game was first slated, no one could guarantee to fill the stadium. Tom Richmond, whose firm handled publicity for the event, recalled how the response was immediate and unbelievable. Tickets began selling the last week in August, and a week before the game, only a few $25 seats remained.

On the day, Yankee Stadium was a veritable cauldron of excitement, the stands crammed to capacity, the cheerleaders and marching bands and popcorn vendors adding vim and colour and energy to the game before it had even started. It was quite the build-up. George Nock 'had never seen so many Black people going into a stadium in [his] life'.[10] Grambling assistant coach Doug Porter said he would 'never forget when we came out of that dugout for the pre-game warm-up. This wall of noise hit us and we had never heard this kind of a roar come from a crowd and I looked up into the stand and I saw all of these people, the stands were just filled with people of color.'[11] Meanwhile, Grambling quarterback 'Shack' Harris recalled the dizzying sense of excitement of 'coming out of the locker room, taking the field, noting the sportswriters, the cameras everywhere'.[12] The noise level increased by many decibels as game time edged nearer, with the cheers and the blasting notes of the band melding in one huge cacophony, while the sensory overload of the overwhelming barrage of sound was matched by the bright phalanxes of colour, with the supporters of Grambling sporting black and gold, and Morgan in their orange and blue making it a vibrant spectacle, exploding like so many fireworks on the retina.

Raymond was similarly overwhelmed.

> It was amazing. You know we were just like in awe. You were stepping out in an iconic stadium, an historical stadium. It was Yankee Stadium, the most important stadium in the world. This was Babe Ruth, Mickey Mantle, Joe DiMaggio, Muhammad Ali, and it gave us, as aspiring young athletes, a chance to be seen by the whole world. No one could deny what they saw on that field. So the stage was set, and I can remember our coaches telling us how important it was that we were getting the opportunity to display our athletic

ability, team-wise and individually, on the biggest stage in the world. And then when you add that it was two Black historical colleges for the first time, it was an even bigger stage. So the press coverage was enormous; it was unreal.

That unreality was certainly felt by Grambling cornerback Delles Howell, who seemed to slip dimensions as he walked into the stadium feeling it was no longer a dream. Reality was now kicking in, and it was time to play ball.

For Grambling, the sheer magnitude of the moment could not overshadow one unfortunate reality. They would have to start the game without their star quarterback: No. 14. James 'Shack' Harris was nursing an injured ankle to the extent that before the game, he couldn't put his full weight on it. This was a body blow, without a shadow of a doubt.

Things careened from bad to worse as the game got underway. On Morgan State's opening possession, quarterback Charles Harrison hit Raymond streaking down the field for a forty-eight-yard touchdown. Raymond remembers it almost as a divine intervention. 'They threw the ball, and for me, I was thinking "please let me catch it," and I wasn't worried about being caught because I could run and once I caught it, it just worked out that way.' Delles Howell's main memory, unsurprisingly, was a gut punch of disappointment that it wasn't on his side; it was on the other side. It was an eye-opener to him and a shock at the same time, but it also meant that he knew they had come to play. Grambling assistant coach Doug Porter was similarly rocked by the fact Morgan State scored as quickly as they did. He could see that everybody at this stage was still jittery and twitchy, still getting the feel of the game itself, which set them back on their heels.

The Morgan State Bears jumped to a 7–0 lead, a crushing psychological blow in any team sport where one side takes a commanding lead right from the off. It was a key moment but far from a decider.

Grambling struck back late in the second quarter on a big play of their own. Filling in for Harris, sophomore quarterback Frank

Holmes connected with wingback Frank Lewis for a thirty-three-yard touchdown, tying the score at seven-all at the halfway mark.

Raymond recalls, 'The feeling was, oh man, here they come, because we knew they had a great team, and if we could keep it to a low-scoring game, we felt we had a chance to beat them, but it was a little demoralizing when they came back to score.'

All still to play for, tension racked even higher.

3.

HALF TIME

After the Grambling Tigers' Marching Band entertained the crowd at half time, the third quarter got underway. It became apparent that this was going to be a slug fest. Someone from Morgan State Bears was managing to break pretty much every one of Grambling's runs – grabbing a shoe, a heel, as if there was an extra man in play.

The Bears kept mostly to the ground, with the backfield duo of John 'Frenchy' Fuqua and George Knock gaining 138 rushing yards on the day. But the defenses would not relent, and the score remained tied at seven points each early into the fourth quarter.

The Morgan State coach had a way of lifting his players' spirits, of urging them on. As Chester put it: 'Coach Banks had a way of elevating the situation to the point of just urgency. He could motivate people in a way that is rare.'

The clock showed there were ten minutes left of play, with Grambling punting deep in their own territory. Raymond Chester was about to change the game again, this time on the defensive side. Coach Banks had grabbed him and, despite the fact that he had had a fabulous game as tight end, now found himself playing defensive end. This was one of Banks's more inspirational substitutions, even though it was far from the only one of his career. Raymond stormed across the line and blocked the punt. 'I decided I was going to block the kick. And I went back there, leaped up and, boom, the ball rolled through the Grambling end zone for a safety, putting Morgan State in the lead 9–7.'

This made quarterback James 'Shack' Harris antsy, jitteringly eager to play, almost to the point of pleading to be put into play, to be let loose. As the game went on, he started warming up and kept asking the coach to let him start a series. At six foot four and weighing in at 215 pounds, it must have been difficult to refuse his request without fear of repercussions, especially as here was a player widely touted to be the first Black quarterback to make it big in the NFL, where the position was normally white, with very few exceptions.

Grambling assistant coach Doug Porter had been badgered by Harris all through the game, the super-keen player insisting that, given a chance, he could get movers down the field and they could score. It was clear that something had to change, so Harris was put in.

The Grambling star quarterback was clearly hobbling, and the first five passes were incomplete. But then the offense started to gel and the Tigers began to roar.

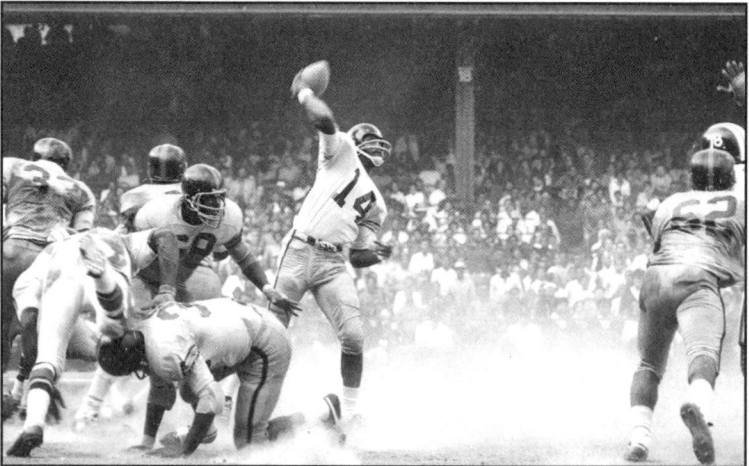

Grambling State quarterback James Harris (14) in action, passing vs Morgan State (Photo: Tony Triolo / *Sports Illustrated* via Getty Images)

Raymond Chester was now part of a team on the back foot as the Shack asserted some authority despite his injury. 'He came in limping, and then he proceeded to march down the field throwing the ball around like throwing darts, and I don't think we particularly played what we call a prevent defense, but it felt like it was prevent defense because they marched straight down the field.'

The Shack stepping onto the field certainly changed the dynamic. When he came into the huddle, it was almost like a new game. James 'Shack' Harris felt that if he could get back in the pocket and find his feet, he knew he had a good offensive line. All he then had to do was hobble back. Unfortunately, hobbling isn't one of those verbs you want to use in a needle match set amid a sea of adrenaline. You need super-fit players playing to the very edge of their ability.

With a well-orchestrated balance of run and pass, the Tigers chewed up the clock, zip, zip, zip, and got up to the Morgan Sate ten-yard line, ready to pounce, setting up a first and go with one-twenty to play.

Raymond knew that he and his teammates had to dig in deep now, look for inner steel and resolve. 'The crowd was going crazy, and by this time, everybody was pretty tired because it was toward the end of the game and we were just desperate to hold on.'

After a two-yard loss on first down, Grambling went to the air, and Harris found Lewis cutting to the end zone. The ref signalled them down at the one-yard line.

Grambling was stunned by the decision, believing the ball was well and truly grounded. As a result, Delles Howell maintained that Grambling players would go to their very graves believing that Frank Lewis scored when he was tackled down on the wide.

The clock was now seemingly acting as an extra Morgan State defender. With just thirty seconds left, the Grambling fireplug of a fullback Henry Jones took his 235 pounds up the middle but was met by a solid wall of Morgan State defenders. Frantically trying to quieten the crowd, Harris signalled a timeout with a mere four seconds remaining.

With so little time remaining, the decision was simple and stark. Should they go for field goal or touchdown? That decision essentially lay in the quarterback's hands. The coaches had game-shaping opinions too, of course, and Doug Porter felt that Morgan State wouldn't, couldn't hold out again, and that was the decision made on the sideline, that if they wanted to win, it had to be a touchdown.

It was down to one final play, therefore. Even the seconds on the clock felt shorter, tighter somehow, possibly because of the adrenaline coursing through tired veins. The win was tantalisingly close. Grambling needed less than a yard; the line itself was within arm's reach. Fingertips away.

Eddie Robinson sent his offense back on the field for fourth down, and Grambling dug in deep, once again, for one last push. The call went to Jones to wedge right, and as a consequence a ton and a half of beef crashed head-on. The ball had gone to Jones, who disappeared under an agitated scrum of bodies pushing hard down about the line. It was a huge collision of bodies as Raymond and the entirety of the Morgan State defense hit into Jones and the Grambling offensive line. There was little clarity about what was going on but plenty of pandemonium. One official shouted that it was a touchdown. Another match official disagreed. Henry Jones added his voice to the chorus of voices disagreeing. But the second official's view prevailed. The uncertainty lasted what felt like many minutes, which for some of the dog-tired, exhausted and depleted players must have felt like centuries. Doug Porter backed Jones's opinion as he thought Grambling had got in. The players on the field thought so too, but the officials thought they hadn't. And, of course, the referee's decision is final.

So the team was denied success even at this last-breath attempt. The match officials disentangled the mass of bodies to finally agree on a verdict, and at this point the crowd was uncommonly silent, as if someone had died. Here were sixty-four thousand Trappist monks who had each taken a vow of silence in place of the raucous, sometimes rancorous fans.

At long, long last, the referee held the ball above his head before tossing it into the air. The silence was shattered with whoops and hollers and many thousand hoots of joy.

View of scoreboard and fans in stands
(Photo: Tony Triolo / *Sports Illustrated* via Getty Images)

In sport, the way you lose speaks volumes about you. Being sportsmanlike, Delles Howell concluded it had been a great game and suggested you had to give Morgan a lot of credit because they didn't hold Grambling one down but held them four down.

It might have been a crowning moment, the sort of career-high that stays with you all through your life. But sport has its ironies and Raymond wasn't party to any of the last-minute drama even though he played a central role. He had been rendered completely unconscious, so left the field completely unaware of the thunderous ovation he was being given.

When everyone else was celebrating the Morgan State win, I was in my room, in bed, being seen by a doctor because I had a big lump on my head because I got knocked silly on the last play. All these guys were talk, talk, talking, but the fullback, a 235-pound guy, well, he and I met in the backfield and I was knocked silly. That play happened on their side of the goal line. We met full-on, heads boom. Those who say they scored are nuts; they're completely wrong because we made contact on their side of the line.

So, as the crowd, or a half of it at least, went crazy, Raymond stood up in a daze, even as a big knot took shape on his skull. His recollections are fuzzy, as you might expect, but he recalls a bag of ice on his head and a doctor escorting him to the sideline and then on to a bus. Once back in the team hotel, the medical advice was to stay in bed, use another ice bag and take some medication. So Raymond failed to share in the uproarious post-match excitement: 'My dad and my brothers came up to the room and spent some time with me – to see if I was ok – but they had to drive back home that night because they'd driven up that day to see the game, but they came to the hotel because they were concerned about me. I did not do one thing to celebrate.'

As you might expect, Raymond's father's natural pride that day knew no bounds.

> Oh my goodness it was karma. My father had piled into a car and driven up to New York with one of my brothers and a sister. They drove all that way and they weren't going to be able to stay in a hotel because they couldn't afford to. They came all that way, saw the game and then came to see me because I had been injured. Having waited around to see the coach and the people in charge, they found out where we were staying and came to my room, this had to be hours after the game, then drove all the way back to Baltimore, maybe four or five hours' driving in his 1966 Dodge – six cylinder, plain light blue, the only new car my dad ever bought.

That detail about the automobile in question is very much a feature of the time: this was the age of the car, and a vehicle could signal a great deal about the owner, as Raymond can attest.

'I'd saved my money and bought an old Ford, maybe a '57 Ford, an old car like that. I'd had some trouble with it, having to have it fixed and so on. And when I started going to Morgan, my dad *gave me his car.*' That act of generosity speaks volumes about the sort of relationship Raymond had with his father:

I can't tell you what that meant. The only new car he ever bought in his life, he gave me the thing because he was proud of me. And he took my old raggedy Ford which I'd pieced together.

One roommate of mine, he had an old car that didn't have a battery, but I had a car with a battery but it wouldn't run! So we would take the battery out of my car and put it in his. The guys would ride in the car with me. When I finished Morgan, I gave it back to my dad who then gave it to my sister. It really was the family car!

The papers summed up Morgan State's victory crisply with headlines such as 'Grambling coach takes blame for vain TD try'. Here was a coach who would accept full responsibility both for his team's performance and defeat.

James Harris has confronted that decision many times since, re-running it in his mind as if on a tape loop. Any time football experts asked him about the field goal, and they asked a lot, he would suggest that if you played for the man he believed to be the greatest coach to ever live, all you ask him to do was call the plays he believed in and that they had practised.

Raymond Chester thinks the win went against the form of the respective sides. 'Grambling probably had a better team than we had, and this was proven in games after that: we never beat them again. We were just on a mission that day, and I think we were inspired; we played more inspiring football on the day.'

It was more than an inspiring game; it was a cultural and racial shift. Eddie Robinson's biographer, Richard Lapchick, was of the opinion that the game was definitely a statement about being Black in America and that while white people had Woodstock, Black people had this game, and they were both love-ins.[13] Doug Porter believed one of the things the game did was tell America that HBCUs played good football and had outstanding athletes. It was also a matter of deep pride for Earl Banks, who opined of his team that they had made him proud of them.

That September afternoon in Yankee Stadium was an opportunity for people to see the cultural significance of historically Black colleges and universities and how well they played football. It was also a time for many individuals in the city to celebrate a truly terrific game.

Raymond's friend Mel Harrison, a lifelong football fan, saw the game as a seismic shift.

> Black athletes were thought of as another class. Black people were not accepted as athletes. They were revered – up to a point. A Black athlete was performing, in a way. But there was all this underlying stuff. I mean people would pay to watch a Black athlete, but they still wanted to restrict Black people from some parts of society and some of its benefits.
>
> Admittedly, there was the Negro League and the Harlem Globetrotters – the Globetrotters were a constant – people would go to see them. The football was confined to the South with mostly Black colleges, which connected with the Black migration from the South to places such as Detroit and Chicago. When you have two Black historical colleges playing in Yankee Stadium, all these people who have migrated or had family that moved from the South – it was kind of like a reunion. It wasn't long before that that a Black person couldn't go to a baseball game. When Jackie Robinson played baseball, a lot of times Black people couldn't go to the stadium. A game like that, Morgan State versus Grambling, for the championship was like a kind of acceptance – we're here now. We're accepted now. This is New York.[14]

Morgan State running back George Nock suggested that New York moment just went to show how much the Black community was starving for a showcase, for that type of ball play, and that they would have supported it every time.

This one big game led to many others. It was like lighting a fuse. Other cities and their stadiums all but begged to have teams such as Grambling come pay a visit. They saw it as a money maker. The Grambling football team and band went on to entertain crowds across the US and, indeed, across the globe, even playing the first intercollegiate game in Japan in 1976.

But it wasn't just entertainment. 'They put Black college stars on display for pro football scouts to see,' as Raymond Chester puts it. It was an awesome experience and crucial showcase of footballing skills. 'None of us had ever played anything like playing in front of sixty thousand people in Yankee Stadium. It gave us exposure that many of us used to catapult us into a professional career.'

The NFL and AFL (American Football League) teams would draft an astonishing thirty-one players who were on the field that day. Black college football and its exceptional athletes could no longer be ignored. Schools across the country, even those in the segregated south, began to recruit from the same talent pool.

In an ironic twist, that trend toward integration would undermine Black college football's own level of excellence and lead to a diminishing in Black college football standards. Players were tempted to go to other schools which had better resources and could make better offers. It was also damaging to the academic attainment of young Black athletes. A lot of the major programmes didn't insist on academic rigour as keenly as they did on the athletics side of things. Coach Eddie Robinson, like many coaches in a similar situation, knew at the time it was going to be harder for him to retain quality players, admitting that while he was definitely all for integration as a Black man and as an American, he was not quite so enthusiastic from the point of view of a football coach. He knew he was going to lose players to the blandishments of better-resourced colleges. Which he did.

Something was lost along the way to integration, as BCF historian Michael Hurd has argued. 'Black college football is still around, still has the bands, and it still has the connections between the alumni and that shared history in the Black community but in terms of what it was pre-integration it's not going to be that again.'[15]

Though integration took its toll on Black college football, the Invitational Football Classic grew and prospered and was still going strong half a century and more later.

After defeating Grambling in 1968, Morgan State continued its winning streak to thirty-one games before suffering its only loss of the season. Earl Banks retired five years later and was enshrined in college football's Hall of Fame in 1992. With fifty-seven years as Tigers' coach, Robinson sent over 200 players into the pros, and with 408 victories, he is still the coach with the most wins under his belt in Division I history. The Grambling team became known as 'the team that will travel', and that match exposed the young players to opportunities to go to places that they probably would never have dreamed of going.

That was a deep and enriching life experience for them: such young men never would have been to New York had they not been members of the Grambling team or the Morgan State cohort. For Raymond Chester, the game was a central defining event in his life. 'Going to New York, playing in Yankee Stadium, it was the biggest thing in our lives.'

For the Yankee Stadium crowd, many of whom had travelled from afar, it was a captivating, prideful, indelible moment. It even became an urban myth, with people believing they had been there when they had not or imagining a vastly exaggerated scoreline, with even another side winning the day. In truth, every ticket had been sold, with a crowd numbering 60,811. Maybe that last one, that final digit, was eight-year-old Craig Spencer whose uncle took him and his brother to the game. 'That was my first experience of seeing HBCUs play and I was just amazed to see sixty thousand plus African Americans at that game.'[16] Ten years later, Spencer would himself be a player, after winning a scholarship to play defensive back at, wait for it, Morgan State University. There, Spencer avers, the place made him a man.

The stands emptied and the clearing up started. It had been a great display on field, and the gladiatorial contest had been fought without blood, well not *too much*. There was a big TV audience, too, as it was aired on WCBS in New York. There were other spin-offs as well. The game raised over $200,000 for the New York Urban League's educational initiative, with the lion's share going to the street academies and the rest into a scholarship fund which would eventually fund 200 places for young people at university.

Raymond wears the memory of that day with pride.

So we pulled it off. The game itself...what happened to me...I had some opportunities in that game, and man, I just made the best of them. So it was a fabulous game for me and a fabulous spotlight for me, but I was more excited that the whole thing came off...first of all the fact that sixty-eight to seventy thousand predominantly Black people filled that stadium. They traveled from all over the country, and there was not one incident, no incidents of fighting or riots.

The scoreboard at the end of the Morgan–Grambling face-off recorded a winning margin that wasn't huge but was none the less categorical, marking Morgan State's triumph. And all the points were scored by Raymond, who with customary humility plays that down. Other, lesser, players might make much more of the fact.

The game was extremely close and well played, and we managed to beat Grambling. I managed to have a great game both offensively and defensively; I scored all of the points for the game, which is in my mind the least of the most important things about that game. There were questions answered that day. How do we make people understand and take a hard look at the educational opportunities and all the positive things that are happening at these predominantly State-funded historical Black colleges? So that was kind of the goal and to get some recognition for the coaches and the staff and provide opportunities for the staff so they could move on to the pros. So good schools. So the year we played that game we had eleven guys off of our team drafted to go into the pros. It's a huge number of guys. Somewhere like Alabama would have that nowadays, or USC might have that now, but in 1968 that was unheard of. And then it was an opportunity for the two schools to probably split a six-figure gate, which was also unheard of.

This game was played during a period of meagre college budgets and a dearth of scholarships and most of those that were available were a hodge podge of, say a teacher's grant, a student loan, a federal grant and athletics scholarship all pieced together to provide the revenue for one young athlete to go to school. Raymond recalls:

> I don't think we had more than two or three scholarships in the college, so it had to be piece-mealed together. I had a job, some kind of maintenance for the college, cutting grass and so on, I had work study, had a teacher's grant… Everything was contingent on your grade point and being eligible to play because if you didn't make your grade point and weren't able to play, you lost what financial aid you had coming from the athletic department. So it wasn't a free lunch.

Raymond rightly balloons with pride when he shares the fact that Morgan is now in the top ten engineering schools in the country and has a tremendous reputation both academically and in athletics. Some of that success has roots in the Grambling game: 'Part of the impetus for that game was to generate more publicity for the schools and for their athletics program and generate money. Probably each school got $50,000 to $75,000, which was a huge amount of money at that time. So those were some of the things we got out of it.'

In a 1960 speech called *The Rising Tide of Racial Consciousness*, Martin Luther King had described doors which 'were opening now that were not open in the past, and the great challenge facing minority groups is to be ready to enter those doors as they opened'.[17] Doors were certainly flung open after the Grambling versus Morgan State encounter, with so many players on the day being drafted into the professional teams. The game was a cultural high-watermark and a commercial success, and it brought dozens of players to the attention of an NFL that had only recently merged with the AFL. That September day in the Bronx saw barriers broken. Some were in the process of being done away with for good.

INTERLUDE:

BALANCE

Noun.
Definition. An even distribution of weight enabling
something or someone to remain upright and steady.

As a student, one of the subjects that really appealed to Raymond
was kinesiology, the science of movement.

> Especially balance. That's the thing I tried to achieve more
> than anything as an athlete, perfect balance in movement,
> but you learn to appreciate the beauty of movement of the
> human body and strength and balance and leverage. You
> see a lot of that in professional sport, but to most of the
> world it's overlooked. When you look at dancers, when you
> look at ballet, the artists are phenomenal athletes. I mean
> the things they do with their bodies and the things they're
> able to do, the positions they're managing to do over and
> over again, the jumps and the splits and so on. I have a
> tremendous respect for ballet dancers most certainly.

Raymond believes that balance is very important for a footballer, even above power and strength.

> Balance is the key to everything, balance and strategic movement and leverage. Understanding the center of gravity and where your leverage is. The guy who has the better balance in football generally is the guy who ultimately wins, balance and range of motion and consistency in that.
>
> In football it looks like a game where – 'boom' – the guy who hits the hardest and the biggest wins, but it's not. It's the guy who hits the hardest over the longest period of time, so it's not who hits the hardest but who hits the hardest the longest, over the duration of the game and over the season; those are the teams that win.

Raymond can look at football as one big ballet, in which you can:

> Look at a guy that weighs 330 or 340 pounds, can run and pirouette, then fall and be up again in an instant. They can knock someone off their feet, over and over and over again, be in tremendous contact and impact, and most of the time, they get up and dust themselves off, go back to the huddle and get ready to do it again. Now if you took average human beings and you had them collide with the force and the speed that these guys do routinely, every play there'd be tremendous injury; it would be blood and guts and stuff everywhere. Most of the time you have these tremendous collisions and pileups, and everybody gets up and everybody's ok. Nobody's mortally wounded.

Raymond can see all these pirouettes and pileups as a very special kind of dance.

> The coach is the choreographer. The coach comes up with the master scheme, the master game plan, the overture if

you will, for the whole thing. Then there are the individual coaches, they're also choreographers. Most pro-sport, basketball and football particularly are choreographed, they really are. Baseball is more of a reaction type thing, action-reaction, action-reaction, and there's a lot of that in basketball and football too, but there's a lot of planned choreography, you know, I'm going to move here forcing them to move there, and then I'm going to spin and go to the area they've vacated. This requires a lot of practice, and most time spent practicing is dealing with footwork – where I'm supposed to be and when and where am I meant to be in coordination with where all the other players in the team are going to be or where the opposing team are not going to be. Yes, a lot of choreography.

The instructions come from coach on radio to the quarterback. Right now, the quarterbacks have receivers in their helmets. They're meant to be controlled by the referee so that instructions stop just before the play is implemented, but when they're in the home, the coach can tell them things. That wasn't true in the past.

For Raymond, balance is the thing, a paramount skill.

Physical balance…being a wrestler, you need to have tremendous balance and leverage and center of gravity and footwork. All those years of wrestling – years that I hated – was a huge part of what made me such a good football player. I also had that discipline, that will to win and also that willingness to accept the responsibility that whether we won or lost was in my hands. I was never going to blame someone else for losing because I was the man who wrestled last, and the crowd was there and if we lost, I was there in front of them, and it was utterly humiliating. On the other hand, if we won, I was a hero.

There's a YouTube clip of Raymond that shows the apparent power of his running as players come at him from all directions, trying to bring him down.[18] But he shrugs them off like flies.

> I've had a couple of plays like that in my career, and I've seen other people have them, and I have to be honest, when you catch the ball and you're in the open and you start to run, there's a certain adrenaline lift. There really is, and when you add the adrenaline pump to the momentum and the weight, the size and power and direction, then it can be fairly difficult for people to bring you down. It's all a matter of leverage and so on, and people would prefer to be able to trip you down as opposed to throwing you down or knocking you down, and I liken it to a rugby scrum. I kept trying to fall down, but every time I was getting ready to fall down, they hit me and straightened me back up, so don't overestimate that – that most of that was due to the fact they wouldn't let me fall. They just kept on hitting me and hitting me, and we went thirty or forty feet down the field like that because they wouldn't let me fall.

It's one hard way to make a living.

PART TWO:

HOW A LEGEND IS BORN (AND BROUGHT UP)
1948-69

4.

FAMILY LIFE

The hero of this book, Raymond Tucker Chester, was born on June 28, 1948, in Cambridge in Dorchester County, Maryland, subsequently growing up in Baltimore, at 83 Washington St. 'I have nine siblings. There were no fewer than six kids at home at the same time – my sisters, my brothers and my mom and dad. For the most part there were probably nine or ten of us living in the same house as my eldest siblings moved away.'

Raymond describes his mom, Bertha, as 'A brilliant mother. She first got pregnant when she was fifteen, then got married, had ten children and despite all the demands on her time continued to live a full life, which mainly revolved around religion.' Faith was very much in the family: Raymond's grandfather on the maternal side was a big-time Methodist minister in New Jersey and New York. Bertha became a minister in the Baltimore Washington Conference and then an associate minister at Elmhurst United Methodist Church in Oakland. She wrote hymns, collected in the volume *Songs of Faith: Then and Now*. One of them, 'I'll Always Put My Trust in God' (Psalm 125:1), is dedicated to 'my beloved son, Raymond T. Chester, Sr. Please Dear Lord, let my son always remember the full significance of the truths in this song. Thank you for Thy great love towards us as a family. Help me always to be worthy.'

The lines of the hymn run:

> Years ago I used to wonder
> Just how my life would be
> But the answer came back quickly
> Just put your trust in Me.

Bertha was not only a woman with a strong spiritual side to her; she was also pragmatic and full of common sense, which she was happy to share with her son. 'My mother gave me motivation and sound financial advice, covering basic things such as "work hard, save your money and invest your money".'

She also introduced an element of competitiveness into the family, as Raymond recalls.

> What she thought she was doing was using me as an example. I thought it was putting me under undue pressure and on my siblings because we all had different abilities, desires and capacities. I felt she should stop doing this; I didn't want my siblings to dislike me, that I be seen as the favorite son. I wanted her to stop doing that to me, to keep making comparisons.

Considering the way that competitiveness was introduced into the family, and given that sport is, at its heart, all about competition, it's somewhat surprising that Raymond is the only sportsman in the family.

> I had a brother who was a brown belt in karate, and another went off to the service and he became pretty good at shooting pool. His dream was to be a professional gambler. He was my older brother, Ivy Junior, who was murdered in Detroit. My brother Tim went to college, to Lincoln University, and became a vice cop in Baltimore. He was a

good cop, dedicated to really trying to do the right thing, but this caused some problems because there were others around him who were at various levels of corruption. It was a pretty challenging situation. Then there was Michael, who was the baby of the family.

The history of America is one shot through with convulsions, as the chains of slavery were broken by abolition and the bloodletting of the Civil War. Raymond's family did not stand apart from any of this. The Chester family originally travelled along the underground railroad, the network of clandestine routes and safe houses for escaping slaves, established in the United States during the early to mid-nineteenth century. It was used by enslaved African Americans, primarily to escape into free states and sometimes north into Canada. As Raymond explains, 'Harriet Tubman the abolitionist's place was some fifteen miles from my grandparents' farm. The route of the railroad led north to Pennsylvania and Boston, to New England and whatever.'

Family is paramount in Raymond's life. Raymond's grandfather John Wesley Chester, born in 1876, was named after the great English Methodist preacher, John Wesley.

My grandfather lived on a rural property at Church Creek, Golden Hill, Maryland. My dad was Ivy Henry Hooper Chester, the best man I ever knew in my life. Absolutely. My dad was very, very special. If I could sum him up, he was a man who would make any sacrifice for his kids or family. He would give you the shirt off of his back and not be expecting to get a return on it.

My grandfather's mother and her brother were slaves on the same property that my grandfather eventually owned and where our farm was built. The story goes, as my grandfather told me, that his mother and her brother were slaves, but it was a different kind of slavery. They were sharecroppers – they didn't own anything, but they were able to work on the property and they were able to establish a household on land that was owned by the landowner or the slaveowner, if you will. In return, they had to pay a bounty, grow crops or raise crops to benefit the landowners.

So, the Civil War happened, and my grandfather's mother's brother left to join the Union army and was also killed there, in one of the negro battalions. The next of kin got a sum of money to compensate for his death, about fifty dollars, so my great grandmother took the money and then she gave it to the landowner for safekeeping. When she wanted it back, he didn't have it to give. So in lieu of the money he gave her about ten acres of land, which was a pretty good deal, and my grandfather was born there and also my father was born in the same place as well as all of his siblings. My grandfather amassed about seventy-five acres of land in total, and that became the home site, the farm and the truck patch, and we all worked there. In that area there's a place called Hoopersville. There were the Spicers, a big family, and it is my belief that the land thereabouts was owned by either the Hoopers or the Spicers.

When Raymond first explained where his grandparents lived, he told me it was in tidal Maryland and then paused, as if he'd have to explain exactly what he meant. But I happen to know the area well, having once written a book about Smith Island, which is part of a marshy tidewater archipelago that includes Hooper's Island, a crow's hop from Golden Hill. It meant that when we were having dinner one time in Wales, I was able to reach behind me to the shelf and gift Raymond a leather-bound history of Maryland, which actually included references to Hooper's Island and the area where this side of his family farmed and lived.

Raymond often visited the farm and spent hardworking summers there, learning lots of different skills. From the age of eight or nine, he learned how to drive a tractor and hitch horses, to slaughter hogs and chickens, saw how to grow crops and harvest crops such as corn, field corn, tomatoes and soya beans, and also learned how to build things and dig ditches.

Raymond with his father (Courtesy of Chester family)

Raymond's father, Ivy Chester, was the very definition of hardworking. He grafted in heavy industry as a steelworker but, as if that wasn't enough, he had a second job as a cab driver. This was a pattern that would be repeated throughout his working life, keeping two jobs in order to feed what was a big family. Despite those two incomes, Raymond still recalls a childhood of poverty and yet suggests they never went hungry or needed clothes or shoes, even if the shoes and clothes they did have were resolutely second hand. 'Lots of times we ate cabbage, or spaghetti or mackerel cakes, but we also experienced some good things – rice pudding, bread pudding and occasionally a ham. We ate hot cakes and corn bread and then more cabbage, but we always had something to eat.'

Raymond's early childhood had its tribulations and trials.

When I was about five, we were living in Cambridge, Maryland, and my dad found a job in Baltimore, and he began to commute from Cambridge to Baltimore, which is a three-and-a-half-hour drive just to work, terrible. His cousin Amos Stubbs had found him the job, but he died in a terrible accident while commuting, so my mom and dad decided they needed to move the family to Baltimore. My father and my older sister and older brother moved first. My second oldest sister Rachel was left in Cambridge with close friends of our family who didn't have kids: she was adopted, basically.

I was handed off to an aunt and an uncle, Lata and Adam Prattis: I was literally given to them at the age of four or five. They were going to raise me. That was dramatic for me. I cried and cried: I hated it. It didn't last very long for me because every time my parents came to visit, I just pissed a fit, crying, so finally my dad just said, 'You know what, I can't do this to my son anymore; we're taking him back to Baltimore.'

The city of Baltimore could be a tough place.

Looking back, where I grew up was a hellhole, literally. Anything that was happening was happening. Any movie you've seen about New York or Philadelphia, it was going on. They were mean streets. And it was clandestine to the point where the block where you lived – a two-or-three-block square – was the extent of your domain, and when you went out of that into another block you ran the risk of anything happening. To even date a girl that lived a couple of blocks away was dangerous. And so protecting yourself, being able to fight, to run, that was just automatic. To fight with fists, that is. Fortunately, when I was young it was fists, but as I got older and time went on, people were getting shot and stabbed.

On the streets, size was on Raymond's side. 'Luckily people leave you alone if you are big, and they did leave me be. Because I was bigger, it meant that I was invited to play baseball or football with the bigger guys.' At the time, Raymond associated with young men who were all some five years older than he was. His best friend at the time, Joe Barber, was the same age, and as a consequence, they were both marks, the nominated victims of pranks and ruses.

There were these eight or ten guys that were five or six years older, so we got picked on non-stop, all the time. We were always getting initiated into one thing or another. In order to be 'in the club' you had to cut all of your hair off, in order to be 'in the club' we had to do this or that...

The challenge was to try not to overreact, not be predictably violent and try not to be a criminal, or aggressive. And I was getting that sort of message at home. You know my mom and dad were sweet people. They taught us to love in a time of hate and violence. They taught us to be benevolent in a time of extreme poverty. They taught us to be self-reliant, and my dad taught me more than anything to be calm, to stay calm.

Much like his father before him, Raymond grew up with a very strong personal work ethic. Hard graft seems to be very much in the familial DNA. He had his first jobs early on in life. 'I worked as far back as I remember: I was either working or aspiring to work. It started with the realization that people would pay you to wash their steps, or cut their grass, or shovel the snow in the winter or carry their bags at the supermarket.' He could be ambivalent about his age when it suited him. 'So, when I was seven, eight or nine years old, I would put my age up to twelve, and at twelve up to fourteen, and venture out to far-off neighborhoods in the winter to shovel snow.'

One can picture the young boy determinedly walking through rain and stubbornly trudging through snow to earn a dollar. There was one very long walk to a country club, a distance of over ten miles. Raymond could earn two dollars for carrying golfers' bags around the course, then hand the numbered clubs to the players as and when they asked for them. If he then claimed to be older than he was, saying he was sixteen, not only could he caddy but he could work in the kitchens too. Like father, like son, Raymond thus worked two jobs, caddying on the course by day and being a busboy or dishwasher in the clubhouse at night. As he crisply puts it: 'I knew work.'

5.

HIGH SCHOOL DAYS

Did I ever tell you researching a book is hell? It often involves having skilled mixologists creating perfect cocktails so you can make sure your subject is entirely relaxed when you turn on the microphone. A long research session might involve two or even four drinks. Like I said, it can be hell, a testing business.

'There's game in almost everything we do,' suggested Raymond one afternoon in Luka's Taproom and Grill in the city of Oakland's Uptown district, where we were quietly enjoying a couple of margaritas. He often comes up with such bon mots, little slivers of philosophy, or maybe just the result of thoughtful tequila sipping. Around us, office workers came in to decompress after a hard day at the keyboard and chatted amiably against the background plinking of pool balls. Sadly, it's a bar that has since closed down after twenty years in business, not able to survive the changed post-pandemic world in a downtown where determined retailers share space with the homeless. It's a sad loss in a city I have grown to love deeply, a gritty, genuine place which I got to know and appreciate in the company of my father-in-law, Franklyn, who was a great guide to its places, its pulse and its bars. Just as is Raymond Chester.

Over a contemplative *añejo* tequila, Raymond conjures up his high school years, when he excelled at more than one sport.

> I could run, and I'd found that I was pretty good at team sports, especially football and some track events. I was captain of the track team, and my sports were the shot put and the discus, but I also threw the javelin. As a matter of fact, at one point in high school, I broke the record for both the shot put and the discus at the same meeting. I was pretty prominent there, but being one of the captains of the team meant I had to do a lot of things. If we needed to have someone run the 220 meters, I'd run it, or if they needed someone to run the mile I'd do that, or pole vault: I'd do all that stuff.

Raymond attended Frederick Douglass High School in Baltimore, established in 1883, at a time when the school system was segregated. Originally named the Colored High and Training School, Douglass happens to be the second oldest US high school created specifically for African-American students. Prior to desegregation, Douglass and Paul Laurence Dunbar High School were the only two high schools in Baltimore that admitted African-American students, with Douglass serving students from West Baltimore and Dunbar serving students from East Baltimore.

Frederick Douglass himself was an inspiring figure. An escaped slave, he became an American social reformer, abolitionist, orator, writer and statesman. Indeed, he became the most important leader of the movement for African-American civil rights in the nineteenth century, the sort of man who fully deserved a school being named after him.

A sense of the spirit of the place is prevalent in a speech once made at the school. On June 22, 1894, a year before his death, Frederick Douglass gave a commencement address at what would become his namesake school, saying:

Frederick Douglass High School, Baltimore (Photo: Eminonuk / used under
CC BY-SA 4.0, https://creativecommons.org/licenses/by-sa/4.0/)

The colored people of this country have, I think, made
a great mistake, of late, in saying so much of race and
color as a basis of their claims to justice, and as the chief
motive of their efforts and action. I have always attached
more importance to manhood than to mere identity with
any variety of the human family...We should never forget
that the ablest and most eloquent voices ever raised in
behalf of the Black man's cause were the voices of white
men. Not for race, not for color, but for men and for
manhood they labored, fought, and died. Away, then,
with the nonsense that a man must be Black to be true to
the rights of Black men.

Segregation was a fact of life when Raymond was growing up.

I remember when I got to Baltimore, I was in between
the age of starting school and kindergarten and first grade.
I never went to kindergarten and then started from first
grade – in the mid to late fifties. That's when I really first
understood segregation and racial discrimination.

All of the schools were segregated, the swimming pool was segregated, restaurants were segregated, buses were segregated, but at that age it didn't seem like a big deal to me. I was accustomed to it. There would be a white water fountain and a Black water fountain; restaurants were commonly named White Coffee Pot, White Castle, White this or that, and they meant precisely that. There was a white beach and right next to it was a fence and right next to it there was a beach for Black folks...and Jewish folk. At the time I was too young for it [to] have any real significance for me, as I was in my world which was a Black, Afro-American world. On my mother's side there was a high level of education, people who were educated either in seminary schools or church schools. In fact, many of the schools, particularly the historical Black colleges, were started by churches or religious groups. But the education that came out of them was really good, with teachers who really insisted on attendance and the best effort and that kind of thing. And I'd started myself being home-schooled by parents.

At high school, Raymond realised that football was his destiny.

When I was a high school player, I didn't have one of the glamour positions – I wasn't a running back or a receiver or whatever. I was actually a tackle, a blocker, and on defense I was a defensive player too, so I was kind of a grunt, a lineman. And then I started to realize that people were scouting me, recruiting me to play football and to wrestle. So I got recruited by the University of Maryland on the Eastern Shore, by Notre Dame and by quite a few schools on the East Coast. It's interesting because some of them wanted me to play football, and some wanted me to wrestle. Because wrestling was big on the East Coast – at Penn State and Lehigh in Pennsylvania and at Maryland – and so I was recruited as a defensive player, a lineman and a wrestler. And then there was this one invite by a school that was trying to recruit me as an offensive player, as a tight end, coz I had had a little bit of experience in catching the ball when I was in the high school, you know scoring the touchdown. I got a taste of that glory – getting the touchdown and hearing the roar of the crowd – and I determined that I wanted to be an offensive player, to play football and that I wanted to be a tight end.

In the end Raymond accepted a scholarship to Morgan State over such perennial football powers as Penn State and Maryland.

At Douglass High, Raymond shone in many sports. He was an all-conference defensive end in football, placed third in the state in wrestling and was a record shot-putter and discus thrower. It all helped attract attention, and underline his all-round skills.

He loved football much more than he did wrestling, which he absolutely hated.

Practicing for wrestling is a job for grunts. I mean it's a grunt job; it's a miserable job where you sweat. We practiced in a small room that had tile walls, and it would get so hot in that room, and then they would turn the heat up, make it hot so that we would really sweat. There was perspiration and water dripping from the ceiling, and you'd have these wrestling tights on, and you'd be stinky and sweaty, and it was miserable. And there was so much pressure on you as a wrestler. Competitions were tough. You're seventeen years old and you've got the weight of the world on you as you're wrestling last. I was wrestling heavyweight, which means I was weighing 215 pounds and I was wrestling guys who were 300 pounds, something like that. We had a good wrestling team, and the outcome of the match came down to you.

Wrestling, being tough, hard, stinky *and* sweaty gave Raymond reasons enough to hate it.

I always dreamed of being a basketball player, and also I
was a very good football player. Our football coach was
also the wrestling coach, and one of our football coaches
was also the basketball coach. So every year I went out
hoping for a place on the basketball team, thinking I had
played well enough, but I would see our wrestling coach
talking to the basketball coach, fixing it. And the next
thing that I knew I was cut from the basketball team and
on the doggone wrestling team.

Due to his size, Raymond found himself wrestling in the heaviest
weight category.

I had tremendous height spurts from the ninth grade
through the tenth and eleventh grade. I was measured at
six foot four and a quarter, and when I was weighed for
wrestling in high school, I weighed in at 215 pounds, so
wrestled as a heavyweight.

The thing about wrestling is this: it's a team sport,
but it manifests itself in individual effort and individual
matches. So at heavyweight you wrestle last. And it's
popular...wrestling crowds in my high school were as
big as the basketball crowds, and we had a pretty good
wrestling team.

His most memorable experience was wrestling last in a big meet, an
away game where there was the added challenge of competing in a
strange space, in someone else's gym.

The matches were close, so it came down to whoever
won the last match; they would win the meet. And I
can remember going out on the mat and getting myself
into a bad position where I was about to be pinned. My
opponent had me on my back, but I was bridging because
both shoulder blades have to be flat on the mat in order to
be pinned, and I was struggling for all I was worth, trying

not to be pinned, and I could hear the crowd roaring and stomping and clapping and clapping and clapping and clapping. Finally, the referee hit the mat as I was pinned, and the whole gymnasium exploded. People jumped up and were screaming, and they carried the winning team off, and I was on that mat having been pinned, having been utterly humiliated in front of all those people, having lost the match for my teammates. I can remember how bad that felt, and I've never ever forgotten that, and I made a vow that day that I would never allow myself to lose in that fashion again. One of the most memorable and impactful experiences of my life was being pinned and losing that match and suffering that humiliation.

Losing in this humiliating way was an important life lesson for the young man and one he would never forget.

6.

MORGAN STATE

As we know, after high school, Raymond resisted all the blandishments and enticing offers from a clutch of universities and plumped for Morgan State, in his native city.

Founded in 1867 as the Centenary Biblical Institute by the Baltimore Conference of the Methodist Episcopal Church, the institution's original mission was to train young men in ministry. It subsequently broadened its mission to educate both men and women as teachers.

In 1915, Andrew Carnegie gave the school a conditional grant of $50,000 for the central academic building. The college met the conditions and moved to its present site in northeast Baltimore in 1917. Morgan then remained a private institution until 1939. That year, the state of Maryland purchased the school in response to a state study that determined that Maryland needed to provide more opportunities for its Black citizens.

Morgan State had been playing football since 1898, or thirty-one years after the school was founded. The team's all-time record is 405 wins, 379 losses and thirty-eight ties. There was a golden era, as 173 of those wins came between 1929 and 1959 when Edward P. Hurt was the head coach and the Morgan State Bears won fourteen CIAA championships. Hurt and his assistant coach Talmadge L. Hill built a solid programme that allowed Black athletes to showcase their talents where such a venue had been non-existent before. Later, Earl Banks won four CIAA championships during the 1960s and an additional championship in 1971 after Morgan entered the Mid-Eastern Athletic Conference (MEAC).

Banks succeeded Hurt and took Morgan football to the next level. Banks was the head coach from 1960 to 1973, coaching the Bears to a thirty-one-game winning streak, through three unbeaten regular seasons, winning four CIAA titles, a MEAC championship and four bowl games. It followed that thirty-five of Banks's players would go on to play in the NFL.

Its history wasn't the only reason Raymond accepted Morgan State's offer.

> First of all, Morgan was a historical Black college. It was a small school, with a total of about twelve thousand students, but it was also a very, very fine school…with high academic standards and a great reputation sportswise, in the fields of football and track and field.
>
> For instance, our track and field coach, Eddie Hurt, coached the 1964 Olympics team – he had a gymnasium named after him. Our football coach in his own right was just as legendary: there are few coaches in college ranks that have been better than Earl Banks. So more than anything else there were two things that I wanted when I was trying to figure out what I wanted to do. Number one, I wanted to stay on campus: I had lived in a house where there was twice the number of people as there was room, so I wanted a place on campus.

Raymond also wanted to be an offensive player, having got a taste of the limelight and savoured the joy of scoring touchdowns.

So the majority of the teams that had been wooing me wanted me to be a lineman, at which I was very good – they wanted me to be a defensive lineman or an offensive lineman. One school, when I met with them, offered me the opportunity to play tight end and live on campus. Morgan offered me that while the others didn't. I went to all the others; they sent someone to get me and paid for the trip, but they wanted me to wrestle and play defense. I decided to go to Morgan, got a room on campus and played offensive. I didn't know that I'd end up playing both offense and defense. There's never been a day of my life when I've regretted it. It was as fine a college experience as I'd hoped to have, in every aspect – socialization, education, the athletic experience – I would not change it for anything.

Raymond started at Morgan in 1966 and went from 1966 through 1970, when he was drafted to play football. But graduating did not go smoothly.

The funny thing is, I didn't get my degree in 1970. There's a class you have to take when you start your studies called 'freshman orientation', which tells you how to use the library and helps familiarize you with the school. I didn't see the need to go to it, so I just cut the class, the whole semester. So anyhow I flunked the class.

Fast forward to when it's time to graduate. I've got a pretty good average, you know, not great – 2.7, 2.8 grade point. I'd never had a problem with school; I just never wanted to be anywhere other than in the middle of the pack and I was not going to fail ever. I flunked freshman orientation and half of an art class where I didn't like the teacher.

When it came to graduation, I had good grade point, but I had failed art class and the orientation, so they wouldn't let me graduate, even though I had way enough credits. So I got drafted by the Raiders and went off to Oakland to play football and then had to go back. I had to go back to

Morgan in 1971 and pass the two courses, including half of one in art. It was hilarious; it was just crazy. You needed something like 123 credits to graduate, and I probably technically had 130, but it wasn't enough – in Morgan you had to have the requisites, you had to. So my degree says '1971' even though my class had graduated in 1970. I had gone to play football for the Raiders, number one draft choice, made the All-Star team, was made Rookie of the Year and then spent the off-season going back to Morgan. Learning the use of the library! Go figure.

When he was chosen for the Raiders, it wasn't just the fact that Chester combined size and strength, making him the best possible example of the virtues and prerequisites of an ideal tight end. It was his versatility that caught the eye of Ron Wolf, the Raiders' director of personnel operations.

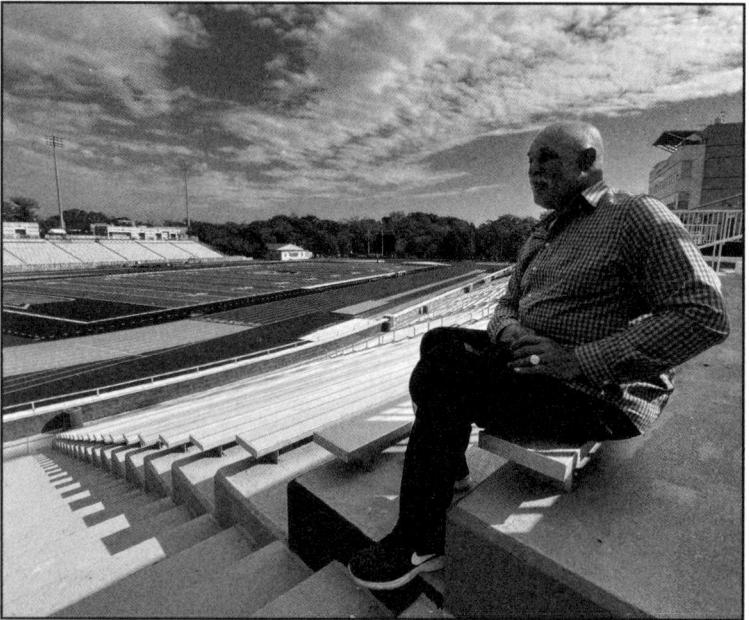

Return visit: Raymond at Morgan State, October 2023
(Photo: Martha Hill)

Although he set Morgan State records for receptions and yards gained, Raymond had worried about where he'd be drafted. 'I was actually disgusted with the college season I had. I was kind of worried about the draft.' By his reckoning he was at 100 per cent in only one game in his senior year.

That game was Morgan State against Texas Southern in the Astrodome in Houston. Ron Wolf was in the stands and was thoroughly impressed at Raymond's varied skills. In that game he returned a kick-off sixty yards, and Raymond played wingback, tight end, wide receiver and running back, underlining how much Morgan State thought of him.

Actually, the Raiders were surprised that Chester's name was still on the board until their twenty-fourth pick of the 1970 draft. During the seven seasons he played for the Raiders, he had made a major contribution to the success of the Silver and Black.

To those who'd seen him develop, it was hardly surprising to see Chester excel on the football field. He had shown his ample athletic ability early on.

As a collegian, he had returned a kick-off ninety-five yards for a touchdown and was on the receiving end of his school's longest pass play, seventy-eight yards.

> I played offense and defense and scored all the points as we beat Grambling 9–7. I caught a fifty-yard touchdown pass and then blocked a punt which went out of the end zone for a safety. I had fun that day.

He recalls one game during his rookie season that didn't start out being much fun at all. The Raiders were playing in Detroit against the Lions on Thanksgiving Day. Chester was going against crafty veteran linebacker Wayne Walker.

> He was killing me, tripping me down, grabbing my facemask and just doing things that cagey veterans do to rookies. The late Jacque McKinnon, one of our tight ends

that year, pulled me to the side at half time and talked to me about being aggressive. Out of that talk came my use of the arm-swing and head-slap techniques, which at that time tight ends didn't use.

Aggression, being tripped, facemask-grabbing, arm swings and head slaps – they are all part of the steep learning curve facing the rookie player, who lives and grows via experience, learning from each and every game, be it as a player or as a spectator. You play, live and learn. And then play again. You get your head slapped. You slap a head in return. Life lessons that hurt.

Being on the field in football is an education in itself, an unwitting enrolment in the school of hard knocks. And Raymond would have many tough lessons to learn as he embarked on his NFL career as a Raider.

INTERLUDE:

IMPACT

Noun.
Definition. The force with which one thing hits
another or with which two things hit each other:
e.g., The impact of the crash destroyed the car.
The bullet explodes on *impact* (= at the moment
when it hits something).

If you walk around the Bay Area with Raymond, you'll have to get used to your progress being a bit stop-start. People are forever stopping to shake hands in San Francisco or fist-bump him in Berkeley. Often one of them will venture an opinion of his ability, such as verbally saluting 'The best tight end ever', which will elicit the broadest Chester smile, even though he's heard it all before. He is always courteous and gracious, remembers what the fans gave him. And he argues simply that it's always good to be appreciated. But that instant recognition isn't confined to California, or even the United States for that matter.

On a winter visit to Wales, Raymond toured the impressive Norman castle at Chepstow before heading for lunch in a nearby pub. As we walked into the snug front bar of the Five Alls, with its real fire and big oak table set squarely in front of it, the barman identified Raymond immediately, even though Oakland is five thousand miles away. He promptly fed some new logs into the flames and got us sat down. I'm not even sure we paid for the opening round of drinks. Raymond is well known, much loved and his athleticism and playing prowess appreciated on at least three continents, as a recent visit of his to Mexico City confirmed.

The Five Alls public house was an ideal, convivial setting for discussing sport, or rather comparing sports: football and rugby. (It's interesting, but certainly not sobering, that so many of our conversations have taken place in bars, pubs and drinking clinics such as the Murenger and the Beverley in Wales and the sadly now defunct Luka's Taproom and Grill in Oakland, not to mention the bar at the Oakland Municipal Golf Club, where Raymond is codirector, near the city's international airport. We also had a long day of sipping tequila and contemplative beers at the Lake Chabot Golf Club, when rain whipped across the greens outside and it was good to be indoors.)

For many years, Wales was known as a brilliant rugby nation, and although football – which some call soccer – has become increasingly popular and now rivals rugby as Wales's national sport, there is no doubting the deep passion for rugby, for watching thirty men battling for control of an oval leather ball.

On international days, especially when Wales are playing at home at the Principality Stadium in Cardiff, the streets are awash with supporters dressed in red, carrying leeks, dragons and other Welsh national symbols. They're as committed a bunch as Raiders fans in their black and silver regalia, and they share a similar enthusiasm for beer, with pubs in Cardiff sometimes running dry should the home team win, especially if it's against arch-rivals England. Wales and England have lots of previous history, much historical abrasiveness, you might say. It's a long story, going back to the death of Llywellyn, the last native prince of Wales in 1282.

Some say that the eighty minutes of rugby played between the two nations each year in the Six Nations Championship is still a matter of settling very old scores.

Raymond and I blow off the foam from our pints of bitter and start to compare sports. There is much overlap of agreement. Both American football and rugby are notoriously physical games, matches of brute strength and high impact and the question 'Who hits harder?' has torched many a fiery debate between fans and sportswriters alike. There's no doubt that both sports are tough as can be, physical to a fault and then some. We could expand the discussion to compare the two types of rugby, rugby union and rugby league, but then things could get even messier.

Size certainly matters. American footballers can be big, or often really big, some of them weighing as much as 300 pounds or 136 kilograms. Raymond was 232 pounds or 105 kilograms. Now, the average weight for someone in a New Zealand Super Rugby team is 108 kilograms, so they would be far from a pushover, other than if you were driving a bulldozer. So, although American footballers can sometimes fit into the body size category marked 'extreme', on average, the sizes of players in both sports are not that dissimilar, especially since rugby players started to work on upper body strength and to bulk up.

But when big men hit or crash into other big men, you have to reach for special, scientific language to measure the degree of impact, namely 'g-force', which many people know from watching science fiction films. It's the thing that makes the astronaut's face scrunch up as she or he accelerates in movies such as *Top Gun: Maverick* or *The Right Stuff* as pilots or astronauts open up the metaphorical throttle. In technical language 'g-force' is a measurement described as the type of acceleration that causes an accelerating object to experience pressure acting in the opposite direction. The units of measurement of such acceleration are gs, where one g equals the force of gravity on the Earth's surface, which is 9.8 metres per second. Just to give you a sense of what a few gs feel like, plunging down an average amusement park rollercoaster will exert a force of anything between 3 and 6 gs on your body.

Rugby players can often take hits that are more than 10 gs many times over the course of the game. Meanwhile, American footballers might experience an average tackling force of more than 25 gs, although the padding helps absorb some of that. Work that out in rollercoasters and it's pretty lurching mathematics, underlining just how hard and impactful these hits actually are. American footballers can look like modern-age gladiators with their helmets, shoulder pads and lower body protection, including shin pads, all in total weighing up to 10 kilograms.

Before a game, an American footballer will don shoulder pads, elbow pads, forearm pads, as well as other padding to protect the hips, thighs and knees. But it won't stop there. Raymond, like his fellow players, would spend a fair bit of time before any game getting wrapped, protected and padded.

On this modern Samurai warrior's feet there'd be socks, tape as well as play shoes, while the basic uniform would include pants, girdles as well as supporters around the groin. There'd be lineman's gloves and of course the distinctive head garb of both helmet and face cage. When the last of these came in, they fair unsettled some players. Raiders' wide receiver Bob Chandler found them 'a little terrifying since most of us were used to wearing a single bar'.[19] But even these were limited in the protection they could offer when a linebacker crushed into Chandler, resulting in his nose gushing blood and his lower lip being nearly ripped in two.

Raymond has quite a collection of helmets in his home set in the redwoods of the Oakland Hills. It's like the Raymond Chester Helmet Museum, and he could probably charge admission. You can see the various design adaptations over his playing lifetime, the shapes of both helmet and face guard changing according to prevailing sports technology and design, a hint of style and fashion combining with a lot of precision protective engineering.

An American footballer is pretty much known by the helmet and face guard: it really does give a player the look of a Samurai in a *kabuto* helmet, prepared for battle. They're not unique, though: sports such as ice hockey have something similar, of course.

Legend, or history, or a subtle mix of the two, has it that the football helmet dates back to 1893. Admiral Joseph Mason Reeve had apparently been hit in the head so many times that his doctor was predicting one more hard knock would surely lead to instant insanity. So Reeve promptly visited a shoemaker and asked him to make him a helmet that would last – please forgive this most specialist of shoemaking puns – and so was fashioned a hat made of moleskin complete with matching earflaps. It saw duty for a brief spell in football, but Reeve also took his prototype across to the US Navy where paratroopers used them when dropping through the air during the First World War.

The idea of head protectors in football caught on slowly, and as a consequence some players were sporting soft leather helmets in the 1900s, upgrading to hardened leather by the 1920s, but even then only some players wore them as it was a matter of choice rather than edict. Helmets weren't actually mandatory until 1943, following the first use of the plastic helmet in 1939, which introduced a crash-test-dummy look into the sport, although the scarcity of plastic during the Second World War was a problem in the supply chain. Even when peace broke out, the quality of plastic necessary for the helmets was in short supply and they could often break on impact, leading to the NFL banning them while this worrying aspect was sorted out. Then some padding was added to the insides. Protection of the player was an evolutionary process.

The next addition was artistic rather than protective, when, in 1948, the halfback for the Los Angeles Rams Fred Gerke decided to paint curly ramshorns on his helmet, thus ushering in the age of the helmet emblem, and thus a competition to find the coolest decals. Nowadays, you have the five-pointed star of the Dallas Cowboys, the bald eagle's head of the Philadelphia Eagles, the rampant lion of the Detroit Lions, the horseshoe symbolising the Indianapolis Colts and the modernist deconstructed falcon with splayed wings and outstretched talons representing the Atlanta Falcons.

But the helmets, while protecting the skull and the ears, did nothing to stop the players being given black eyes big enough to resemble human pandas, while noses were bloodied or broken and swollen lips were commonplace.

The evolution slowly continued. A single bar, fitted like a facial guard rail to protect the nose, eyes and chin, was used from 1955 onwards and invented by Paul Brown, the coach of the Cleveland Bears.

It came about because of a key moment in a single game. Brown very much wanted to keep his starting quarterback Otto Graham on the field despite the fact the gifted player had taken a very hard knock to the mouth. Brown swiftly rigged up a crossbar, and after Graham had received the necessary medical treatment, he was ushered back into the game. The new helmet addition was soon adopted by the whole of the Cleveland team. Brown then promptly patented the design. Some people resisted the development, of course. Former Detroit Lion Garo Yepremian was the last of the diehard NFL players to appear without a face guard, stubbornly refusing to wear one until 1967. He did regret it, mind. In a TV interview with ESPN he admitted that he would wake up every morning after a game with blood in his mouth. Single bars gave way to more elaborate structures such as the ones players wear today.

But protection is still not enough. In his book of recollections of *Violent Sundays*, leading receiver Bob Chandler's list of injuries sustained during his career is cautionary. He recalls knees aching from the high-speed torquing or being crunched in a tackle. He also describes how his chin had required six stitches after being torn open, how one of his front teeth was knocked out, and how both elbows had been so bruised that he had to have fluid drained out of them every week. Then, one day, his lung burst after being hit in the back with a helmet while stretching out for a high pass. He 'thought the impact had knocked [his] heart loose'. It's what happens 'when very big men charge into you at forty miles per hour with no intention whatsoever of slamming on the brakes. The body ends up as a car wreck.'[20]

PART THREE:

NFL CAREER 1970-1981

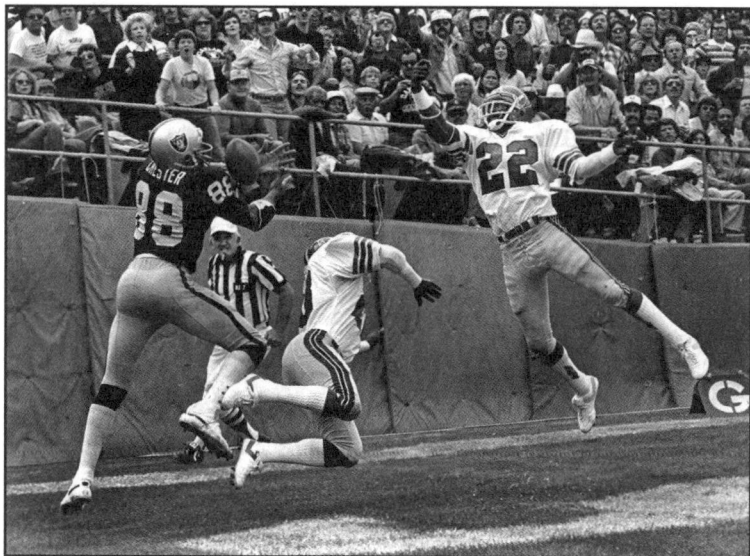
Raymond hauls in a touchdown pass against #22 Rolland Lawrence of the Atlanta Falcons, 1979 (Photo: Ron Riesterer)

7.

ON BEING A RAIDER

'Is it the greatest team ever? My Badass Raiders of the '70s?
To me it was.'

(John Madden)[21]

The Raiders of the 1970s were the very stuff of legend. As Al Davis told writer Peter Richmond: 'There was no team that other teams feared more. No one wanted to play us. That's a sign of greatness… and dominance.'[22]

Raymond has the rare distinction of being one of the few players to have done not one but two tours of duty in the silver and black of the Oakland Raiders, a team described as being in equal parts brilliant and carefree. He played for them between 1970 and 1973, and after five years at the Baltimore Colts, came back to Oakland to put in another stint in 1979.

Fresh out of Morgan State University, the 240-pound, six-foot-four-inch athlete was the Raiders' first-round choice in 1970, and this proved to reap rewards for the club straight away. He caught forty-two passes for 556 yards along with seven touchdowns during his first pro campaign. Add to that the fact that he grabbed a pass at every Raiders game that season, and it was little wonder that he was named All-Pro and Rookie of the Year as the promise of this Baltimore native had been more than fully realised. He felt right at home on a team that had its share of stars and of course was thrilled to learn that the Raiders had made him their No. 1 choice. To boot, he had always wanted to live under the warm California sun and, just to clinch it, if he could have had his choice of teams, it would have been Oakland.

> When I was a kid in Baltimore, we'd be sitting around on the steps talking or playing a game, catch with the ball, and at that time there were these shows that we'd watch on TV, and California was just something on television. It was Ronald Reagan in a Western or it was Zorro or Route 66. It was a legendary place: we didn't know anything about it. So [we] would sit on the steps and sometimes talk about it and say, 'Man, I'm going to get myself a '57 Chevy and drive to California along Route 66.'
>
> And also, because it was this backdrop of the great outdoors, where you could go hunting and fishing with elk and antelope and deer and horses, man, are you kidding me? It was a fantasy land; you wanted to see it. I remember flying to California the first time: I was in shock. I just couldn't believe what I was seeing, just the open ranges and the fields and how much land there was. Wow! It couldn't have been more different if I had landed on the moon in terms of what I was seeing and experiencing for the first time.

He had Al Davis, the charismatic, mercurial owner of the Raiders, to thank for the move to the open ranges and the California sunshine, tempered by the morning mists of the Bay Area. It had the extra pleasure of being an unexpected opportunity. Raymond was not on the list of the top 150 players in the country when he came out of Morgan State as an unheralded college prospect. But Davis saw something special in this big, speedy athlete and made sure they used the club's first choice to nab him.

Davis would wait for the last possible minute before sending a scout such as Marv Marinovich (assistant coach from 1968 to 1970) to check out a player, 'as [he] thought people were watchin' where [he] was goin' and would know who [he] wanted'.[23] In the case of Raymond Chester, that last possible minute was on draft day itself, which was really going up to the wire. But Davis had a name as a strategist, of thinking many plays ahead.

Raymond well remembers the process.

> First of all Al Davis sent scouts to personally assess me and meet me; he sent them just to meet me. The guys spent a whole week with me…they wanted to look at my athletic ability; they wanted to watch me run, play basketball, and he had a fairly decent assessment – was I as tall as I said I was? Was I powerful? What sort of physique did I have? How did I move? How fast did I run? And so he knew that what he was about to do was taking a tremendous risk, and people were just waiting for him to fail, to tell him how foolish he was. The other teams had me on their list but very low down; when they reached my name they would draft me, bring me in. Al Davis made guys like me a priority, but he didn't do it in a blind. He did it by doing as much of an assessment as he could. He talked to the coaches, he talked to the other players, he talked to players from other teams and he sent Marv Marinovich to spend a week with me. So he had a real good idea that physically I was everything that they expected me to be.

So Al Davis, with Marinovich's help, was the one who spotted Raymond's incipient talent. Davis was himself a young guy at the time, known for his brains and his aspirations as far as football was concerned. He was instrumental in competing against the established NFL with the little fledgling AFL, and they had an urgent need to find talent and assemble teams that could rival the NFL. Raymond suggests one way they did it.

They went to the Black colleges. We believed that the NFL had definite quotas and positions that were open for competition for Blacks, but there were other positions that were closed. We pretty much knew that. Instead of quotas – you know, eight, nine or ten guys, twelve guys – the rest of them were white. So when the AFL came in, they were trying to compete talent-wise and get to a level of play where the fans would appreciate that level of playing, to develop a style of play that was more exciting, faster, more eye-catching in terms of running and whatever. And then at some point they could challenge the NFL to the championship and ultimately win. And the quickest route to that was to do the unthinkable, go and recruit from historical Black colleges and tap into that wealth of athletes that had never had the opportunity to compete in the NFL.

In some ways this was a big Al Davis experiment, with no real methodology and no real certainty of the right conclusion. Taking a risk on a player. Following a hunch. But it worked, as Raymond recalls. 'Right away, it just boomed; it just exploded and I was off and going. The papers wrote gleefully about how inept the other teams' scouts were, asking how could they miss this guy?'

There was certainly a winning method in the apparent madness. Al Davis's approach to selecting players was, according to his biographer Mark Ribowsky, 'a paleontologist-eyed notion of the perfect football animal'.[24] As Davis was very much an outsider, and certainly not in the scouting mainstream, he approached the business of selection armed with much more than just a gut feeling. There was some science to it. He was looking for a particular kind of footballing specimen and would go so far as to check out any prospective player's *mother*. As Marinovich, who worked for him as a sort of scout-cum-sporting-laboratory-assistant recalled:

He wanted an advantage from the physical standpoint. He wanted numbers to look at, prototypes, and that was way ahead of its time. It's damn near what they're doing now in Russia and East Germany. For instance, offensive linemen had to have larger hips than what most scouts looked for, defensive linemen, bigger hands and slimmer hips, receivers, longer arms.[25]

Al Davis was selecting soldiers for combat duties. Davis was a strategist, who enjoyed reading theories of war. He saw the Raiders as going to war, not just winning games. And it could be a long war, one of attrition.

Veteran sportscaster Mark Ibanez from Channel 2, KTVU, suggests that Davis was happy to choose players who didn't fit the mould.

> From my viewpoint Al Davis was not judgmental about what your résumé may have looked like in terms of toeing the line of society or even the mores of sports.
>
> One of the simplest ways to put it is by looking at standards of male grooming in the Raiders – hair, beards and mustaches, the clothes you wear, that sort of thing. In the seventies it was kind of a revolutionary look, and the players would get on the bus or plane, faking it, with briefcases full of comic books.
>
> Part of that look came from Davis's own self-image. He wasn't a follow-your-leader type of guy; he wasn't a sheep. He didn't look at a guy who was known as a partner, or known as a night owl. Coach John Madden's approach was be on time, respect your teammates, treat people like men. People respond to that. He wasn't a babysitter.[26]

The dynamic between Madden and Davis was based on testing and pushing intellect in the same way that the Greek philosopher Socrates taught his student Glaucon. In Bryan Burwell's biography of Madden, he says, 'It was always business, not personal, unless you wilted under the intensity of the argument.'[27]

At first, life as a Raider was a bit intimidating for the young Raymond Chester, not least when he found himself in competition for a place against former Heisman Trophy winner Billy Cannon, the Heisman being awarded annually to the most outstanding player in college football.

Cannon wasn't the only big name or talent on the training field. Raymond freely admits:

> There was a scary feeling as a rookie, although I felt pretty secure I'd make the team. There was a wide array of talent and personalities within the Raiders. What struck me was the work ethic of the team. I remember clearly working after practice with Fred Biletnikoff, Daryle Lamonica, Warren Wells and George Blanda. It was expected. If you wanted to be a starter or an important player with the Raiders, you worked after practice.

Other players recall the very different and distinctive work ethic in the Raiders. Bob Chandler, leading receiver for the Buffalo Bills and the Oakland Raiders, recalls how 'everything about the Raiders was diametrically opposed to what I'd experienced with the Buffalo Bills. Management wanted forty-five individuals to play well on Sunday. They didn't care if you dared to be different, if you wore thigh pads or hip pads to practice, or if you lined up perfectly to do calisthenics.'[28] Chandler noted how players would work their butts off but show little regard for some aspects of football etiquette, sitting on helmets or practice dummies in breaks from training. Unlike other teams in the NFL, Oakland treated its players like men, with 'no one standing over you and forcing you into a particular mold. Instead you were given the leeway to be whatever you wanted to be, and this was channeled into our performance. We were proud to be Raiders and wanted to do justice to the team that gave us so much freedom.'[29]

When Raymond was edging into adulthood, his father wrote him a letter that is framed on the wall of his home. The ink is fading now, but that's of little matter because Raymond has the whole of it committed to memory. I tested him one day…

To my dear son Raymond, on the occasion of his twenty-second birthday, who has been all that a dad could ask for, a wonderful son, who has been a gentleman in every phase, who has been generous, kind and loving and peaceful and who has made myself, his brothers and his sisters, his mother and I so proud. A sportsman, educated…

'That's the way that the letter starts,' Raymond says. 'My dad was a good writer. It sounds like a speech with the cadence and rhythm of something important. He wrote that letter and he folded it and enclosed it in a small box along with a bible as I was getting ready to go off to the Raiders and start my life.'

He started that adult life in the company of a wife, Sharon, a high school sweetheart he married three days after Raymond turned twenty-one. 'She actually lived next door to me. I guess I was in my second year at college and she was graduating out of senior high school, and we started dating and shortly after she became pregnant and we had our daughter and what a treasure she is, to this day!'

There were pressures on the marriage right from the start because Raymond was away from home a lot of the time. 'You're with a bunch of young men, handsome, financially secure, popular, and women were magnetized to the team. It was difficult being a young man and staying focussed on your marriage, although it wasn't difficult to stay focussed on the family and provide for them. The whole idea of fidelity was a challenge.'

Raymond's friend Morris Bradshaw, who played with him in the Raiders, recalls such challenges, of being young, of starting out.

You were living your dream, at such an early age – because all things come to pass, all things end – it is very hard to adjust to life after. I remember when the league was still in its infancy and a lot of the bad stories you heard about the period were because people didn't have models to follow, people who were going or had gone through the same experiences you were. The core of that was upbringing, how you were raised. You come to a team at that age; they're not family. You're born with family, and they'll burn you just as fast as anybody else. But these relationships are ones you chose, and then you learn there's good and bad with everything. That's what makes it home; you can't just have the good stuff all the time.

But you'd also realize football is a business, and a nasty business in many ways. I think I was four years in before I realized that, shit, our friends are getting cut; our friends are getting traded; our friends are gone. And then you realize it's a hardcore business. Apart from the injuries, there's the mental aspect of the game, and when you make the team, there's injuries that happen. You live with a lot of constant turmoil.[30]

Raymond would join a successful team that would become an uber-successful sporting business. They scared their opponents in addition to playing ferociously well. As Jim Plunkett once explained, 'It certainly wasn't much fun as an opponent of the Raiders. I say that from experience. There was an intimidation factor. The Raiders wore those larger shoulder pads and that made them look bigger. They wore black most of the time, and they looked meaner and scarier. You couldn't get around that intimidation factor.'[31]

One of the things Plunkett noticed when he got to Oakland to play against the Raiders was that 'every time those guys stepped onto the field, they expected to win. It didn't matter who they were playing. It didn't matter how far behind they were with two minutes left. They felt they were going to pull it out. It was so incredible to be around that confidence.'[32]

By the time Raymond joined the Raiders, they had been around for a decade. When Lamar Hunt created the American Football League in 1960, the Oakland Raiders were on the roster of the very first franchises, created in a flurry of activity on the part of people such as Barron Hilton and his Los Angeles Chargers, which then moved to San Diego, Bud Adams with the Houston Oilers, who eventually name-changed to become the Tennessee Titans,

Ralph Wilson with the Buffalo Bills and a group of partners in the Oakland area that included Wayne Valley and Chet Soda.

Some of the changes of city and name can test the resources of a person's memory bank. The Oakland franchise started off in Minneapolis, but the city withdrew from the league after an approach from the NFL which offered expansion there. So Oakland took Minneapolis's place in the early years of the AFL's existence.

But the name of the city in itself wasn't enough to label a team. It needed an extra noun, something which categorically connected with the place, such as the way the Houston Oilers connected with Texan oil, or something dynamic, signifying action or speed, such as the Los Angeles Chargers or the New York Jets.

In Oakland, they invited suggestions for a suitable name, offering the winner an all-expenses-paid trip for two to Hawaii. The winning entry was, incongruously, the Oakland Señors, which sounded more suitable for Florida, with its Spanish-speaking population, not to mention the fact that señor sounded a bit old, too much like senior. Luckily, common sense prevailed, and so the Oakland Raiders were born, playing at Kezar Stadium and at Candlestick Park in San Francisco while practising and living in Oakland.

In the early years, faced with daunting competition from the NFL, the Oakland Raiders took what they could get, signing anyone they could, from former NFL players to ones from Canada where the playing set-up was not as advanced and opportunities were less limited.

Tom Flores has argued that television was key to the success of the Raiders and to their popularity right across the United States. As the team became better and more successful, they were also part of the national television doubleheader: 'All our home games were at 1 o'clock Oakland time, or 4 o'clock back east. So fans on the East Coast or in the Midwest would watch us after they watched the early game. We were on TV a lot on the East Coast, and we became very popular because of that. Back then there weren't a lot of teams and no home satellite games.'[33]

There were also individual reasons for some of the TV success, such as George Blanda, who had gone to Kentucky, and Kenny

Stabler, who had attended Alabama then joined the Raiders, adding to their appeal to an audience in the South.

They also claimed a lot of territory in the Northwest in the period before the Seahawks flew into Seattle. The Raiders played a lot of pre-season games right throughout the area, acting, in Tom Flores' words, as a 'barnstorming group trying to get fans and it worked'.[34]

The fact that the Raiders played well and in some fantastic games certainly helped a lot, and of course there were some landmark moments that made a little bit of television history.

Then there was the Immaculate Reception, one of the most famous plays in the history of the game. It occurred in the American Football Conference (AFC) divisional playoff game of the NFL, between the Pittsburgh Steelers and the Raiders, on December 23, 1972.

With the Steelers trailing 7–6, on fourth down with twenty-two seconds left in the game, Pittsburgh quarterback Terry Bradshaw threw a pass targeting John Fuqua. The ball bounced before Steelers fullback Franco Harris caught it just before it hit the ground and ran for a game-winning touchdown. The play has been a source of some controversy and speculation ever since, with some contending that the ball touched only Fuqua (and did not in any way touch Tatum) or that it hit the ground before Harris caught it, either of which would have resulted in an incomplete pass according to the rules of the day. 'It was absolute mayhem,' recalls Raymond. 'And given the fear that was in the hearts of the officials, I don't think they were going to change their decision.'

The debate about what happened exactly raged for a very long time. Still does. Raymond recalls how 'Frenchy Farqua came into the Raiders locker room, leaned over and whispered in my ear, "You know the ball hit me." I said, "Yeah, I know the ball hit you." He said, "Yeah, it did hit me, but that's the way it goes." And that's a true statement.'

Raymond also recalls the punishing effect of the loss. 'If you could have packaged all the anger and frustration, it would probably have been nuclear. It probably would have been the equivalent to a nuclear bomb.' It was something that would deeply scar coach John Madden, who said the play, that Immaculate Reception, bothered him then and continued to do so and would continue to bother him until the day he died. Meanwhile, Kevin Cook's *The Last Headbangers* cites the play as the beginning of a bitter rivalry between Pittsburgh and Oakland that fuelled a historically brutal Raiders team during the NFL's most controversially physical era. NFL Films has chosen the Immaculate Reception as the greatest play of all time in their *100* series. The play was also a turning point for the Steelers, who reversed four decades of futility with their first playoff win ever and went on to win four Super Bowls by the end of the 1970s.

It certainly ushered in a bitingly keen football rivalry between Oakland and Pittsburgh. The two teams faced each other often enough in the playoffs and during the regular season that it could appear as if both teams were in the same division, helping to ensure that games between them were must-watch moments in the sporting TV calendar.

Raymond well remembers the confusion of those early years, of trying to settle both into a sport and into a place.

At first when I came out here to join the Raiders, I was living in a hotel, then an apartment, and then my wife and daughter came out and we were living in a small apartment. It created challenges. Sharon was a good mother, committed to being a good mother and being a good wife. My life was just starting to explode and things got bigger for me – my aspirations and my dreams and ideas and my exposure and I wanted to expand my world, my whole world. My sense of motivation and achievement changed, and there was so much out there that I wanted to see and do, and I was married to a sweet, hometown girl, sweet and a good mother who had certainly been good to me, but it wasn't long before I realized that it wasn't enough. I had to grow. It wasn't easy. Sharon and I were together eighteen years. Separating was a tough decision for me because I was close to my family.

Raymond's friendships within the Raiders squad, coupled with Al Davis's belief that the team was family, helped forge very strong bonds with some of the other players.

> What I liken it to is that a lot of times, people who are not in this think it's automatic, and they don't realize that it takes a level of effort to establish and to sustain these relationships. When my friend Daryle Lamonica died, I was shocked and hurt, and then his son calls me and says we want you to speak at Daryle's funeral. I did not want to speak at one of my best-friends-on-the-team's funeral. I had done that too many times, you know, but how could I not? So, there were weddings and funerals and grand openings of businesses, especially in later years. Art Thoms got into the laundromat business, Ben Davidson was in the bar business, Gene Upshaw was in the restaurant bar business, Phil Villapiano was in the retail business and Gus Otto into all kinds of things. We all reaped the benefits and rewards of this culture, but it all required work.

Life is, of course, a complex thing. As we've heard, Raymond's older brother Ivy Henry Chester Jr left home, joined the services and travelled around the world and then got killed when he was murdered in Detroit. Another brother had some run-ins with the law.

Raymond fills in the gaps:

> My older sister Gloria is deceased. She was eight years older than me, and she died ten years ago of a stroke at the age of seventy-one. My other sister Rachel lives in Salisbury now.
>
> When you've got family, you've got the good, the bad and the ugly. The good is that I'm in contact with all of my sisters and my brother, and we love each other and we acknowledge birthdays and holidays and everybody's fairly successful now in their adult lives. The bad side, the ugly side of it, was that our parents divorced. I guess I was a teenager when that happened. Divorce is always tough and it's ugly. Initially they

divorced because they didn't get on. My mother was very ambitious, very heavily involved in the Methodist church. She had gotten a degree from college and obtained a doctorate in theology, and she was then very involved in being a minister. My dad was a laborer and was looking forward to having a housewife, someone who was there when he came home. It didn't work, so they divorced. It was extremely difficult for us because neither one of them insisted that we take one side or the other, but you know you do. When you're amid it, you see the pain and the hardship that it caused, and it is extremely difficult for kids, especially when you love both of them. I worshipped my mom and my dad.

Even as a young man, Raymond had to deal with some of life's big challenges, such as his parents' divorce and the fracturing of his own marriage. But as the old saying goes, what doesn't break you makes you strong. And in the case of Raymond Chester, it created a man of strength in so many ways. Breaking has never been an option.

Al Davis, in choosing the silver and black uniforms, perpetuated a bad boy image and let it be known that he welcomed outcasts and castoffs from every other team in order to give them their last chance. So players felt that he had gone out on a limb for them and repaid this faith by putting their all into their performance. To consolidate this good will, Davis made sure they travelled first class, and played it straight when it came to agreeing contracts, thus taking away distractions that could force a player to take his eye off the ball.

Davis's philosophy helped forge a close team, forty-five men from different backgrounds and temperaments, ages and interests, who would get into fights during practice as a consequence of the white heat of competitiveness but then have a drink and a laugh afterwards. These pronounced bonds of friendship turned individuals into a formidable machine that could beat other teams and garner a world championship. The bonds were sporting and social, too, as Davis always hosted a party in the Oakland Hilton Hotel after every home game, underlining the sense of team but also bedding that team down in the wider community.

Despite initial nerves, Raymond was soon shining quietly among the galaxy of stars that filled the Raiders' sparkling firmament in the early 1970s. Deep down, he was thrilled to learn they had made him the No. 1 choice. Like so many men before him, Raymond had done his fair share of California dreaming, and as a consequence would have favoured Oakland sun and its geographical situation over many a rival. In this he was perhaps unconsciously heeding the advice of newspaper editor Horace Greeley, who famously said, 'Go west, young man.'

The American West had long been viewed as a land of opportunity, a Panavision landscape under wide blue skies which could be the making of a man. It was a blessed land and landscape that Raymond's mother appreciated in full, as a verse from her poem 'California, California,' collected in the volume *The Preacher's Little Book of Poetry* attests:

> Mountains, hills and glorious valleys;
> It's sheer beauty everywhere
> As I gaze speechless in awe and wonder;
> I always feel God's presence there.

Some of the players on the Raiders' roster were familiar to Raymond.

In high school I had watched John Mackey. First of all, he played for the Baltimore Colts, who only had a handful of Black players, and I could pretty much name them all… there was Lenny Moore, Gene Lipscomb, Jim Parker, John Mackey himself, of course, Willie Richardson and a couple more defensive backs. There were only eight or nine Black players out of fifty guys. They were our heroes, and John Mackey, from Syracuse, was a great specimen, a great player who really excelled at what he was doing and really knew he was good.

I grew up in the shadow of Jim Crow. It was there in sport, but it was beginning to change because of those guys who were coming out of Morgan and Grambling and were going to the pros and doing really well. Mackey kind of represented that to me; he was a very well-educated, very well-spoken guy and he wound up becoming the president of our union.

Raymond's rookie year was very successful. The twenty-fourth player chosen had nothing less than an outstanding debut season, catching forty-two passes for 556 yards and seven touchdowns. Playing the Denver Broncos in the fourth game of the season, when the Raiders triumphed 35–23, Raymond skilfully grabbed a twenty-four-yard touchdown from someone who would later become a very good friend, the quarterback Daryle Lamonica, resulting in the first touchdown of a very long career.

The very next week, Raymond was up and running again, this time against a team that would become the nemesis of the Raiders, the Pittsburgh Steelers.

The Steelers would gain a brilliant reputation as one of the best teams of the 1970s, becoming diehard rivals of the Raiders and meeting them in a historical playoff in 1972 and three AFC Championship games between 1974 and 1976, as well as a playoff in 1973.

This meeting in 1970 between the two sides was, however, to be a personal showcase for Raymond's ample gifts. He grabbed no fewer than five passes for 107 yards and three touchdowns on plays of thirty-seven yards from Daryle Lamonica and nineteen and forty-three yards from replacement quarterback George Blanda, the latter being a classic.

In a superb passage of play, pretty much perfect in its execution, Raymond caught a screen pass on the field's right side before showcasing his paces when it came to rapid acceleration coupled with a hallmark grace in flight. He ate up the yards, swiftly going through his body's gears to get into cruise mode in order to reach the end line to plant the ball. This was a game where he scored not one, not two but three touchdowns, making it arguably his best outing in that decade and thus helping his team to a solid win of 31–14. Little wonder that he was chosen as Rookie of the Year for 1970 and chosen All-Pro.

In the seventh game of the season, the Raiders were pitted against another side that the fans heartily despised: the Kansas City Chiefs. In this game, Raymond caught two touchdowns of three and eight yards from his close buddy Daryle Lamonica in a game which, frustratingly for both sides, resulted in a 17–17 draw. By that season's end, it had become readily apparent that the Raiders were blessed with arguably the best three receivers in pro football, in Warren Wells, Fred Biletnikoff and Raymond Chester, but this was to be a winning threesome that would only be on the same team for one year, namely 1970.

Raymond, meanwhile, truly excelled as a tight end. The 1970s saw the beginning of a new era and breed of taller, faster tight ends. Ones who could run. Raymond was perhaps the most feared of the era. Big, rugged and physical, he combined substantial size, great strength, demonstrable 9.8 speed, 4.45 quickness, fast moves, great hands and an athleticism up there with the best of them.

His early years for the Raiders totally vindicated Al Davis's hunch about Raymond. He caught forty-two passes for 556 yards and seven touchdowns in his first pro campaign and grabbed at least one pass in every Raider contest to earn All-Pro and AFC Rookie-of-the-Year honours.

This was something he could build on. He caught 104 passes for 1,574 yards and twenty-two touchdowns during his first three years in the league before being dealt to his hometown Baltimore Colts. Raymond Chester therefore had the rare distinction of enjoying two tours of duty with the Silver and Black as they found themselves a tight end with skills and strength, then traded him away – and then traded him back again.

Danny Jones, in his *Heroes of Yesteryear: Pro Football's Dying Breed of Players from a Bygone Era*, offers his very definite opinion that 'Raymond was an outstanding blocker. The tight end of the 1950s and 1960s, once considered a third tackle, and a position of big, slow, lumbering linemen, was parlayed by the Raiders' Raymond Chester into one of grace and speed. Raymond revolutionized the tight end.'[35]

As Jones goes on to explain, this was an era when players like Raymond presented a deep threat, much as players such as John

Mackey of the Colts and the Cardinals' Jackie Smith had done in the preceding decade. The 1970s saw the formation of a phalanx of excellent tight ends right across the NFL, which included Jerry Smith from the Washington Redskins, Russ Francis from the New England Patriots (and latterly of the San Francisco 49ers), Riley Odoms from the Denver Broncos, Bob Trumpy of the Cincinnati Bengals, Charlie Sanders from the Detroit Lions, Jackie Smith from the St Louis Cardinals and both Dave Casper and Raymond Chester representing the Oakland Raiders.

Dave Casper, who would be one of Raymond's principal rivals in the Raiders squad, was nicknamed 'The Ghost', and throughout his career showed a knack for making the biggest of plays. No play was any bigger than 'The Ghost to the Post' when Casper caught a Ken Stabler pass against the Baltimore Colts in a 1977 Divisional Round game, which set up the Raiders for a game-tying field goal. In addition to that play, Casper was the one who scored the touchdown on the 'Holy Roller' play, as the Raiders beat the hated San Diego Chargers 21–20.

Football is a game where statistics count, of course. Author Danny Jones is keen to point out that Chester caught more career touchdowns (forty-eight of them, to be precise) than four comparable players who have all been inducted to the Hall of Fame in Canton, Ohio: Mike Ditka with forty-three; Jackie Smith, who had forty; Charlie Sanders with his thirty-one and John Mackey – considered by many to be the best tight end ever – who has thirty-eight career touchdowns to his name.

Marshalling the statistical case for Raymond being in the Hall of Fame, Jones includes the fact that Raymond had more touchdowns than 1980s Hall of Famer Ozzie Newsome and Kellen Winslow with forty-five. Further crunching the numbers, or maybe crunching with numbers, Jones reminds us that Raymond had more catches (364) even than the great John Mackey, who caught 331 and more catches and receiving yards (5,013) than Charlie Sanders (331; 4,817).

It's little wonder that at the beginning of his chapter about Raymond, Danny Jones asks crisply and trenchantly, 'Why isn't he in the Hall of Fame where he should be?'[36] as he has all the statistics and credentials to earn his place, including winning the 1980 Super Bowl.

Jones goes on to argue that something isn't quite right about this exclusion when no fewer than six tight ends with inferior statistics have been admitted, suggesting this has more to do with politics than anything else. Jones considers the Seniors Committee of the Hall of Fame should rethink their position or at least address the omission of a man he describes as a 'lost treasure'.[37]

Being a successful rookie brought with it many opportunities. It allowed Raymond to meet a wide range of people – many of them sportspeople – and some of them among the best in the world, such as Muhammad Ali.

I had played my first year in the NFL and was the No. 1 draft choice, and I made several All-Star teams and the *Pittsburgh Courier* chose me as the top NFL rookie in the country. They had this big event and picked the top athlete in every sport – boxing, athletics and so on, and I was twenty-three years old at the time. Jake Gaither and a bunch of other athletes were there along with famous coaches, and so I find myself sitting next to Muhammad Ali, side by side on the podium at this big dinner event, and I'm just Raymond Chester from Morgan State sitting next to Ali. We talked and got to know each other over a Friday, Saturday, Sunday. It was huge, and I found it easy to talk to him because I loved him.

Then they put us up in a hotel, and Ali and I had rooms next to each other and so we end up talking some more and he's explaining his philosophy, and I thought it was awesome because he was so regular. I was young, but so then was he and we became good friends, and he would talk to me about the times when he would come to the Bay Area and to Oakland, and that whole experience was awesome. We sat together at every meal. He had a lot of connections out here in the Bay Area. And the thing that I liked about meeting him was he knew what it takes, the stuff inside you need in order to be great. And that translates from boxing to football to basketball to baseball. What I find to be the essence of greatness is very, very similar – the real great guys have a humility, and they realize that they're lucky and they're blessed and fortunate. Whatever the public persona, here's a guy who understands that he's in a very, very special place for a very limited time and is very fortunate to be there.

In the song 'Coney Island Baby', the rock singer Lou Reed remarks how he wants to play football for the coach. A coach inspires players, pushes them on and pushes them higher. John Madden was the head coach of the Oakland Raiders between 1969 and 1978. He was, as Raymond recalls, 'the youngest coach in the league at the time, he was like thirty-some years old'.

Madden coached the Raiders for a total of ten years, and for five of those they were among the least penalised teams in football, even though, paradoxically, he gave them lots of freedom, loosening the leash on them to the point where it seemed as if there was no leash at all.

In his 1986 autobiography, Ken Stabler used Madden as a measuring stick for assessing Al Davis, who had been:

> A successful coach, the commissioner of the AFL who forced the merger with the NFL, and the shrewdest owner in the game, a man who put together teams that had won more games in the past nine years than any other club. In my mind Al was the biggest man in football. And as a guy who worked for him, I kept wishing he would loosen up a bit and be more like John Madden.[38]

Stabler describes Madden as being much more caring and approachable, pointing out that pro football teams were made up of competitors, often guys who had been starring in the game for ten years at different levels from junior high school through high school to college.

They then found themselves in a situation in pro football where not everyone is a star, and indeed many don't even get a chance to play, with half the players not even starters. For the first time in their lives, they backed up someone else and had to work like hell, hoping to get some playing time to prove that they were good enough to be regulars.

The reserves are often unhappy. I know how they feel because I was one of them for over three years. But there were always guys on the Raiders who encouraged me. Many of the veterans on the Raiders did that with younger players. And John Madden was the man who fostered that attitude.[39]

Madden had many, many strengths, but that didn't sit him at the top of the tree in Raymond's opinion.

This is controversial. I personally think that Tom Flores was much better than John Madden. He was an excellent communicator without saying a whole lot. If you asked who was the best communicator, everyone would say John Madden, thinking of him on radio and television or whatever, as he was so dramatic. Madden did have all of the antics, but Tom spoke directly, not using many words, but you understood what he said. You knew he meant what he said, and I think he was brilliant.

Raymond has clearly played for many coaches and certainly knows the hallmarks of a great one.

They've got to be able to understand the science of communicating and that means back and fore. And I think what every great coach understands is that it's very unlikely that he's going to be able to successfully communicate with everybody that's on the team, every guy, every type of guy on the team. He's going to have to recognize who within his organization does a better job of communicating with a particular group of guys, then find those people, call them captains or war chiefs – that's what I call them. You might have a group of five or six listening to you, but only one or two get the message. The language necessary to talk to fifty guys is very different. The key is to find players who can influence other players, say five guys that have a sphere of influence, who can talk to eighteen or twenty of the other guys. There may still be some four or five guys you cannot reach. Coaches can only take it so far.

You learn to read players. You come off the bench and you'll say this man is killing me. Someone might be down on all fours; then he'll pick his left hand up, twitching his fingers, signaling he's going to the left. Those are the sorts of things that players give to each other. So a certain per cent is knowing the nomenclature and all the plays – how to get to a spot in real time, in the time frame allowed and with the other side's players obstructing you.

Any coach working with the Raiders of the 1970s had his work cut out for him.

Ken Stabler, for instance, reputedly studied playbooks by the light of a jukebox. He drank. A lot. He went without sleep. As a classic quote of his has it: 'All I wanna do is drive around in my truck and drink Jack Daniels…and they just don't understand.'[40]

Raiders' receiver Bob Chandler describes airplane flights to the games as lawless occasions when the backs of chairs were pulled down for the seatbelt-shunning players to while away the flight time playing cards. Even when the plane hit a pocket of turbulence, it was as much as the stewardesses could do to get the players to strap in again.

Chandler thought that players travelling together were akin to soldiers on a troop train or sailors on a battleship journeying to war and so should be able to enjoy a period of truce before battle ensued. As it did, week after week during the season.

8.

PLAYING FOR THE COLTS
(OR FIVE YEARS' HARD LABOUR)

Raymond had proved himself very effective as a Raiders tight end and appeared in three Pro Bowls. Then came a bombshell. He was surprisingly traded to the Baltimore Cubs in 1973 in exchange for defensive end Bubba Smith, who would later become an actor and appear in six of the *Police Academy* movies as well as commercials promoting Miller Lite beer. It was a homecoming opportunity Chester didn't exactly welcome. He didn't want anybody to put out the flags.

Writer Hunter S. Thompson went to prison, as it were, to find an analogy for the Raiders of that era when he suggested that hanging around the locker room was akin to 'being in the weight room at Folsom Prison'.[41] Raymond looked to the same source to find a way to describe the experience of playing for the Colts. 'Five years of hard labor' is the way he puts it. It may have been Raymond's hometown, but this was no happy homecoming. 'I went from the most wide-open passing game in football to the most conservative. I didn't catch a lot of passes in comparison with what I did with the

Raiders. I like to say that my time in Baltimore was like five years of hard labor. It was no secret that I wanted to get out of there and return to the West Coast.'

Coach John Madden had objected strenuously to the trade of Raymond for Bubba Smith, the monstrous defensive end. Madden was proved right quite quickly because Bubba, coming off knee surgery, was a dud. After only three games he was benched, and in a year he was gone.

So Raymond traded:

> Open, expressive play for a much more conservative form of playing that gave me little opportunity to really express myself or shine. It was conservative and lackluster, and I hated it. But I still had my work ethic and a burning desire to be a great player, and I tell myself that even though I compare it to a prison sentence, I will also tell people that I played my best football in Baltimore because I had to. Because we didn't have the talent, we didn't have the coaching that I had been accustomed to, we didn't have the understanding of the game, and in many cases, we didn't have the opportunities to play in a way that allowed us to excel.

It might have been really easy in that first year in Baltimore to become resentful. Luckily, Raymond was blessed with:

> Pride and determination, and it was a lot of anxiety and angst, and boy, I tell you, it was a ton of it, and I had to work through that, and I did.
>
> Fortunately, what helped me, I met some great guys, some of the younger players that were there, guys that became friends. It wasn't their fault; they were just there, just like I was, and trying to make it and build something, but we were a lousy team with lousy coaches. So we overcame that.
>
> I had agreed to not make waves, to be a back-up, and said that I would not make plays, would not get in the

newspaper and challenge them and say that I should be starting. I agreed to just bide my time and play.

That first year I sat on the bench, and interestingly enough they had just got Jim Plunkett and bought him from New England, and he was a mess. He was physically hurt and he was dejected because he'd had a terrible time of it there. So he and I sat on the bench together and had very limited occasion to play, except on special teams – the guys that run on and then off after a play is over. So Plunkett and I got to know each other.

Most of his seasons with the Colts might be described as pedestrian, even though he was playing with the totally gifted Bert Jones as quarterback. Poor coaching played its part, but there were probably off years just because of the sheer unhappiness of the situation and of being in a long funk. The year 1973 was a bit of a nadir, grabbing eighteen passes for 181 yards and a single touchdown in a year when he divided playing duties with tight end Tom Mitchell. It was a year when the whole team didn't exactly cover itself in glory, ending up with an embarrassing 2–12 record and fifth place in their division.

A change of head coach in 1975 ushered in a period of new promise, much of it realised by Ted Marchibroda, who would steer the Colts to three divisional titles in 1975–7, although Raymond's touchdown rate was far from what it used to be, or indeed could be. His best game of 1977 came in the season finale against New England when he caught four passes for 122 yards and one touchdown of seventy-eight yards.

Despite conditions being far from conducive, Raymond did see the plus side of returning east to play football.

Oddly, in Baltimore, I played some of the best football of my life. I played harder and stronger there than I did at the Raiders. I was still very, very fit. I'd had some injuries, but I'd overcome those and I just played harder because I had to. I was on a lesser team. When I was with the Raiders, every other player was a superstar, really good players. So I played hard and we played big games, but in Baltimore I had to play hard because the team wasn't very good. I had to play my ass off. It was cold, wet, the team didn't command respect – everyone in the Conference was used to kicking Baltimore around so it was tough. The first year I was there the team won 4–10.

It was such a huge change for Raymond, playing for a struggling team.

When I first went there, I was coming from the mighty Oakland Raiders with Stabler, Tatum and Willie Brown, all the great players. This was a team perennially in the playoffs and in the picture. They traded me to the worst team in the league. Everybody was confused like I don't know what. The Colts were changing ownership: the general manager, Joe Thomas, well, the people referred to him as a nut. They went through four coaches in the first two years I was there. It was a mess. The second year I thought it was the worst experience I had had.

At Morgan State we had lost just three games in four years. We didn't lose. Then with the Raiders, well, we didn't win the Super Bowl the first time I was there, but we were contenders, knocking on the door. And then I got to Baltimore…it was as cold as hell. The whole system was different, coaches yelling and screaming and trying to teach you something you knew was not state of the art.

I thought that was as bad as it got, but the next year we only won two games! I thought, oh shit, I'm going to go crazy. I'll never forget I was getting ready to go to practice and it was fifteen degrees, in November I think, and I'm thinking, oh man, I want out. I was locked into the contract. They gave me a good contract, much better than what I had with the Raiders, and so I'd go back the same year and there was another coach.

There had been some bonding among the players that were there, and there was a good corps of guys that were tired of losing and looking to build some esprit de corps, do some teamwork and stop losing. And we did. We went from two in twelve to winning nine or ten games the next year. I think the guys just bonded and became a band of brothers. They were tired of losing, being laughed at, being humiliated.

We began to ignore the ludicrousness of the ownership. The owner would come in after a game and start throwing stuff. His son is the owner of the Colts now and he's a great owner. Continually making amends for his father. His dad was a rich Chicago man, made air conditioners or something like that.

I became captain of the team. I knew how to play; I knew how to play better than the coaches after what I'd been exposed to in Oakland and had learned there. So I was probably one of the four or five most consistent players on the team, in terms of my ability to play well, even in defeat. We had a corps of guys that talked about best practices and what we had to do.

It wasn't always best practice though.

There's always going to be a guy or two on every team who plays dirty. I'll give you an example. When I played for the Baltimore Colts, we went to New York to play in a game, at Yankee Stadium against the New York Giants. I caught the ball and I was running and a guy grabbed my leg, right, and I couldn't get away, so I could only fall down, or else be pushed down, coz if they've got your leg you're really exposed. They had me and I couldn't go anywhere, and this young guy on their team came flying into me and he just hit me, knocked the hell out of me. The referees were upset and my teammates were upset, but what shocked me is that the guys on the Giants team got up and yelled at the guy who hit me, saying, come on, you don't do something like that. Because I was defenseless and he just whacked the heck out of me. And his own teammates read him the riot act for doing that because it was cowardice. That's the kind of respect I think that permeated the league in the era that I played in. Man, it was ask no quarter, give no quarter, but nobody wanted to be that guy. You were hemmed in and your leg was exposed, and so someone decided to go break your leg. Any of these guys could do that on any number of occasions but decided not to.

The move to Baltimore is still one Raymond views with regret, especially when he considers how things might have turned out had he been able to stay with the Raiders. 'I wish I could have played with Stabler for ten years or so. I could have put up some great numbers.'

But nevertheless, he is still pleased at the transformations he saw and oversaw. 'I suffered miserably the first two years I was there, and in the third year we had a kind of metamorphosis. We went from a year of two and twelve in the second year to the third year when we found ourselves winning our division. In the playoff we lost to the Pittsburgh Steelers, and then subsequently we lost to the Raiders.'

Jack Tatum recollects that specific game between the Colts and the Raiders and Raymond's role in it as 'a great tight end' in *Final Confessions of NFL Assassin Jack Tatum.*

During the 1977 playoff game with the Baltimore Colts, Raymond Chester could have been the difference in winning or losing, but the Raiders won and Raymond's team lost. That year Raymond wore a Baltimore uniform and was the tight end for the Colts. I'm not sure of the reason but he and Bert Jones never got along. Anyway, because of their mutual disregard, Raymond was wide open on several plays but Bert wouldn't throw the ball to him.[42]

Throughout the entire game, Tatum recalls, Bert ignored Raymond, and the Raiders won by six points in overtime. Tatum further remembers another key moment when Al Davis, in his seat near the press box, decided that he needed another tight end and that Raymond was the man.

Raymond is phlegmatic about it. 'We could never get past the Steelers and the Raiders to get all the way to the Super Bowl, but we competed at the divisional level for the next three years.'

But playing his old team – the Colts taking on the Raiders – had to be different.

> Emotionally, yes. You wanted to do well. You know the guys, you know the talent, you're playing against guys you grew up with and competed with them in practice, oh heck yeah, and you really want to show them up. You want to beat them; that's the team you want to beat more than anything. You want to show them up, while at the same time, I realized that the team we had did not match up to the Raiders and the talent that they had. They had so much talent, and more importantly than having so much talent, they had such effective ways of implementing and using it, and we weren't there yet. We had good players and a lot of talented players, but we weren't even in the same ball park as the Raiders.

The Baltimore years were, if nothing else, character forming, just as memories of fumbling the ball can be educative. Raymond believes:

> Mistakes are character building. I remember the fumbles… The thing that sticks in my mind more than anything in thirteen years of professional football is a big pass that I dropped that would have been a touchdown against a key rival in the pros. In that thirteen years I played, I think I had six fumbles, that's with over four hundred receptions combined, but those six fumbles are lodged there, and I think it's been healthy for me, as opposed to focussing and dwelling on all the glory days and glory moments and scoring big touchdowns. The things that have driven me are those not-so-good things.

Character forming they might have been, but that didn't mean Raymond didn't want out.

Raymond's years of exile in Baltimore finally came to an end in 1978 when he returned to Oakland in exchange for both Mike Siani and a high draft choice going to join the Colts.

Raymond had therefore played for the Colts from 1973–7, catching 148 passes for 2,122 yards and eleven touchdowns. He was made available for trade just before the 1978 season and got a call from Madden, his former coach. The Raiders wanted tight end depth behind future Pro Football Hall of Famer Dave Casper.

It was a case of returning to his old team, but one where new players were very much first in line when it came to being picked to play. Dave Casper, 'The Ghost', was in prime position. (The Ghost was named partly after the cartoon character and also because of his open play, when he was as elusive to catch as a spectre.)

Raymond helped facilitate his eventual move back west.

So, we had played the Raiders and lost to them in a big game. There was a tradition that I would go over and talk to the guys I knew. So I was coming out of the tunnel, where players come out, and I ran into Al Davis, and he said how you doing kid? Good game and whatever, and we talked, and at that time I pretty much had come to the conclusion that I wanted out of Baltimore. I just was not happy, and so one of the things I said to him was I'm doing all right and they gave me a nice contract, but I told him, look I'm not happy here and I want out, and you really got to get me out of here. And he said to me, something like, be patient, be calm. I won't let them hurt you – those were his exact words: I won't let them hurt you, just be patient.

And within a short period of time they had arranged a trade to Baltimore, to get me back to Oakland. At that time, Dave Casper was a young player, and he'd had a fantastic year and was a starter at the position at which I also played, and they were very excited and happy about him. So Madden called me just before the season started, and he said he needed to talk to me. He said Al wants to bring you back, and he says we have a chance to get you, but I told Al I need to talk to you first. Dave Casper may have been John Madden's favorite player of all time, they remained great friends.

Raymond well remembers a slightly cautionary conversation about Dave Casper he had with Madden.

Madden said, 'We like this guy playing at tight end and we don't want a disturbance to disrupt our team.' I said, 'Coach, I understand what you're saying. I promise you I will not create a problem. I will compete like hell because you know I will. If it's the difference between me coming back there or staying here, if I have to, I will make All-Pro on special teams. I'll play special teams.' And he said, 'That's what I wanted to hear.' And he said, 'Ok, stand by.' An hour or so later, the trade was done.

And so I came back, and that first year I sat on the bench. I only caught thirteen passes that first year, which was a tremendous setback for me. I mean that the two trade years, when I first got traded to Baltimore, they didn't know how to use me and I had a tremendously low productive year. I caught eighteen balls in Baltimore, and then when they traded me back to Oakland and I'm behind Casper, I caught thirteen balls. So those are two years out of my career...My production numbers would have been off the chart had I not had those two years.

The year 1978 saw the Colts announce they were trading Raymond to the Oakland Raiders for wide receiver Mike Siani, who was the Raiders' No. 1 draft pick out of Villanova in 1972 and a six-year veteran of the National Football League. It was unexpected and a complete shock. The last place Raymond expected to wind up was back in Oakland. He hoped the trade worked out well for everybody, with both the Colts and the Raiders prospering and benefitting from the trade. And for himself, of course.

Meanwhile, in Baltimore, coach Ted Marchibroda explained his thinking, stressing he had to do what worked well for the Baltimore Colts. He knew Raymond did not want to play in Baltimore. Trading was the most viable answer.

It was reported that a Colt source said the team had contacted every team in the NFL except Miami and New England, Baltimore's chief rivals in the AFC East, about Chester. Several teams had appeared interested but the best offer received was for two fourth-round draft choices. That offer was unexpectedly withdrawn by the unnamed team. The Raiders came back with the offer of Siani, which the Colts accepted.

In his five seasons with the Colts, Chester had caught 145 passes for 1,566 yards and eleven touchdowns. His best year with Baltimore was 1975, when he hauled in thirty-eight passes. In his final season, he finished third on the team in receiving behind running backs Lydell Mitchell and Don McCauley with thirty-one receptions for 556 yards. Having put in five years of hard labour in Maryland, it was time to return to California and to the Raiders again, a move which totally delighted Raymond. Even though he'd grown up in the Baltimore area, it felt like he was going home at long last. After all, it was where his family, the Raiders, lived.

INTERLUDE:

INJURIES

Noun.
Definition. Hurt, damage, or loss sustained.

When a game is such high impact, it's little wonder that injuries are many, various and a constant. Raymond sees this as a fact of life, an aspect of the game one has to live with.

> Football players – whether in high school, college or the pros – are often motivated to continue playing after they've been injured. They keep telling themselves as I did that the injury is not that serious, and yet, in their collective hearts, they know that their athletic career is being pared away. They convince themselves they're okay and willing to continue no matter what the cost. That play-at-all-costs attitude has started and will continue until the body can no longer answer the bell.

Raiders' receiver Bob Chandler put it another way, describing football as a game which breaks bones like most people break toothpicks.

Raymond has not been immune from all this.

> I played football for twenty-five consecutive years, going back to high school and college and pros. You can't play football, or rugby, soccer or basketball where there's that kind of contact with grown men and be injury free. So it becomes more an issue of rehabilitation and conditioning and then tolerance and being able to perform with a lesser degree of injury. So now, as we come to the end of NFL season, everybody's hurt. Everyone who's played with any kind or regularity or consistency is hurt. Somewhere they're hurt: a broken finger or toe or sprained calf or knee. Everybody's hurt. Football is really a game of attrition – who can patch up and stay well and perform best under duress. And that's literally what it is. There's no way you can play that game and be a regular player…play seventeen games or whatever and two or three pre-season games at that level and not be hurt in some way…no way. I know of no one in the NFL who's played the majority of games in a season that did not have some injury…it could be a broken finger or a toe, neck or hip or rib.

Most often this is because of the high-impact nature of the sport or stress in the musculature or joints. 'You have to play on through pain. If you're a regular player or want to be considered an elite player, there's no such thing as not being able to play through injury, and that's kind of what determines great players from average players or sub-par players.'

There were bruises and more bruises, but then there were more lasting injuries. Raymond has been prone to recurring ones. 'I have a disposition to have ankle injuries and some groin pulls and strains. Ultimately, I ended up having hip surgery and ankle surgery three or four times. I've had ten operations – three knee, two hip, three ankle, a shoulder and a few other broken bones, such as a broken nose, toe or a finger, that kind of thing.'

Raymond's partner Martha says he is uncomplaining about pain, even though she's sure he must feel more than he admits.

> I recognize that I probably know about 15 per cent of the pain and discomfort that he's experiencing day to day, and 100 per cent of what he complains about is his ankle which is making the opposing knee get ginky sometimes. That was his last big surgery, and it was a success, but the result is not great. The other result would have been walking on a club foot, a fused foot.[43]

Raymond and I are having breakfast on Broadway in Oakland the morning after a troubling on-field incident. Damar Hamlin, a Buffalo Bills player, was in critical condition in hospital after a cardiac arrest on field during a game the previous evening against the Cincinnati Bengals. Hamlin, a defensive safety, blasted Meyers helmet-to-helmet, preventing a touchdown catch in the end zone.

Raymond starts to recollect other serious injuries in games in which he participated.

> I've been in two games where players were paralyzed. One player on our team, a guy called Ray Jameson, was hit, broke his neck, spent the rest of his life as a paraplegic. Jack Tatum was the Raiders' safety and Darryl Stingley played receiver for the New England Patriots, and they came to Oakland to play us in a pre-season game in August 1978. Stingley caught a ball, and my friend Jack Tatum was defending and came up and made a legal hit on him – there wasn't anything malicious – broke Stingley's neck, and he spent the rest of his life in a wheelchair, dying at the age of fifty-five. So it can go both ways, but it's horrible.
>
> I remember John Madden was the coach at the time, and I remember he would go to the hospital and give us reports.

Stingley himself would write in his autobiography later in life that his injury was a primary reason why Madden walked off the sidelines, though Madden never said so publicly.

Raymond is keen to point out that this injury was not the result of foul play.

> Jack Tatum had a reputation for being a hard-hitter, putting in brutal hits against opposing wide receivers, but anyone who knew him knew that Jack was clean. Everybody on our team loved Jack Tatum, and we understood that Jack Tatum was by no means an assassin. They gave him the name, but that whole incident haunted Jack the rest of his life and it negatively affected his career until the day he died. Jack Tatum should be in the Hall of Fame, right now…I love Jack Tatum: he was my brother, one of my best friends. We'd go fishing together and everything.

When the *Los Angeles Times* sent out questionnaires to 440 former NFL players in 1988, they found that 78 per cent of respondents said they had disabilities, while two-thirds of these former pro football players were certain they were dying before their time, balanced by the fact that over half of them would play again, regardless. Former Baltimore Colt Randy Burke told the newspaper: 'I can talk clearly, but ever since football my words get stuck together,' while another player, Pete Gent, said, 'I went to an orthopedic surgeon, and he told me I had the skeleton of a seventy-year-old man.'[44]

Meanwhile, the Jobs Rated Almanac placed the NFL players very low down the list, indeed, near the coal miner working underground when it considered such factors as stress, outlook, physical demands and security in the work environment. The football player only clambered out of the bottom ten when it came to income. In 2002, the Almanac placed the NFL player at the very bottom of the list, 250th out of 250 when it came to being physically demanding.

One is reminded of a line in Welsh singer Max Boyce's song where he exclaims to *Duw* (God) how hard his experience of working in the mines was.

Sportswriter Mark Kram has suggested that pro-footballers will do anything to keep playing, doing whatever it takes to keep the life, with few 'who will resist the Novocain and the long needles of muscle-freeing, tissue-rotting cortisone…'[45]

Kram's article for *Esquire* in 1992 includes a sad list of former players who were seen by those responsible for disability benefits in the NFL, such as the 'young player, depressed and hypertensive, who tried to hurtle his wheelchair in front of a truck (the team doctor removed the wrong cartilage from his knee) to the forty-year-old who can't bend over to play with his children, from the drinkers of battery acid to the ex-Cowboy found wandering in the desert'.[46]

Following pain comes the painkillers. Michael Oriard, in his *Brand NFL: Making and Selling America's Favorite Sport*, highlights the atypical story of the former Denver Bronco Otis Armstrong who, in 1984, was arrested and convicted (then put on probation) for fraudulently obtaining nearly 1,500 Percodan tablets from nine different doctors over a six-month period. Armstrong was addicted to the painkiller after taking pills by the handful to relieve the agony from seventeen upper body fractures during a seven-year career.

In a game that loves statistics, there are some that suggest that the game doesn't love its players. A report from Ball State University revealed the brevity of the career and the physical pain it involves: one out of three players left because of injury; 40 per cent had financial difficulties and one of three was divorced within six months. Many also remembered the anxiety of career separation setting in within hours of knowing it was over.

According to that study, written by the NFL Players Association (NFLPA) in tandem with Ball State, 65 per cent of surveyed players had suffered a 'major' injury, being one which caused them to miss eight or more games. Of that 65 per cent, around half of the players from the 1970s and 1980s stated they retired due to injury. Over 60 per cent of players reported that their injuries had a negative effect on their ability to engage in physical activity, with a 1994 follow-up piece of work revealing that an incredible 47 per cent of athletes suffered from arthritis. There have been other injuries following the advent of artificial turf fields, but the issue goes far beyond the playing surface.

Injuries mean that a team-mate you befriend might be there one week and not the one following. In training camp, Bob Chandler suggested, 'no one wanted to get close to another player in case the guy you befriended was cut or traded at any time. Like soldiers who go into battle ignoring their buddies because of the risk of losing them to a bullet.'[47]

Many of the most serious injuries in the game are ones affecting the head. Despite the helmets, head injury is still a concern in football just as it is in rugby. Former Wales rugby captain Ryan Jones, who skippered the national team no fewer than thirty-three times, was diagnosed with early-onset dementia as a result of the diagnosis of probable chronic traumatic encephalopathy (CTE), one of the worst cases the specialists had seen. It dismantled Ryan Jones's health and his life, as he revealed in an interview with the *Times*:

> I feel like my world is falling apart. And I am really scared. Because I've got three children and three step-children and I want to be a fantastic dad. I lived fifteen years of my life like a superhero and I'm not. I don't know what the future holds.
>
> I am a product of an environment that is all about process and human performance. I'm not able to perform like I could. And I just want to lead a happy, healthy, normal life. I feel that's been taken away and there's nothing I can do. I can't train harder, I can't play the referee, I don't know what the rules of the game are anymore.[48]

In American football, litigation against the NFL has taken the form of a class action by thousands of former players who argue that the NFL didn't adequately inform them about the neurological risks involved in the pounding and physically demanding nature of the game's knocks and collisions. These include dementia, depression, reduced cognitive ability, sleeplessness and early-onset Alzheimer's.

The same is true in rugby, where the World Rugby Union is being sued by players such as Ryan Jones and Alix Popham of Wales, and Steve Thompson and Justin Wring of England. It seems as if in this school of hard knocks, there are some big and important lessons still to be learned.

Lots and lots of tackling is involved in both sports. Hard tackling. At speed.

And it's also wise to bear in mind that it's never one tackle. The rate of tackle is different in the two sports.

Over the course of a season, Jerrell Freeman of the Chicago Bears led the NFL league with an average of just over seven tackles per game. A rugby player such as Robbie Henshaw of Ireland, on the other hand, can tackle ten times or more in a game, just as he did when his team trounced France in the first game of the Six Nations in 2018. And the body collisions in rugby don't just come in the form of tackles, as there are also rucks, mauls and scrums (getting technical on all of these would take some time, so let's just say it's about getting well and truly physically stuck in). In American football, blockers take a lot of hits, but they only play for minutes, whereas a rugby player might be on for the full eighty minutes and is usually only replaced, or substituted, around the sixty-minute mark. During that time, every player might expect to be hit or to have to tackle someone running at him at full tilt or collide accidentally, sometimes when the player is in the air, hoping to catch the ball. Sometimes a rugby player's skull will crunch into another's when they're both high off the ground and therefore defenceless. Concussion is often the result.

Players used to get concussed and play on, in that very different era before concussion protocols when it was said you only came out of a game if a limb had been severed. Some went as far as to say you only came off if it was two, as hard men could hop.

Raiders receiver Bob Chandler maintains that the game changed when the competition to play professional football became more intense. The flood of money into the game put pressure on individual players to stay in the game. 'Which changed the way they behaved. Because the helmets couldn't break, some of them used them as battering rams, their heads becoming weapons on the charge.'[49] The new professionalism and huge injections of cash ushered in the use, by some, of cheap shots and a seeming disregard for causing injuries on the part of some players, even when those injuries could bring a player's career to an abrupt end, and with that the means to look after himself and his family.

Artificial turf was another new problem. This was cheap to maintain and offered a good, clean backdrop for the game on TV, but it could cause horrendous problems for knees and ankles.

The difference in time spent on the field between the two sports is almost as dramatic as what they wear. A rugby player runs an average six miles per game while his counterpart might only run one mile and stay on the pitch for a total of eleven minutes. So NFL players take harder hits but fewer of them, a game of big hard men trying to bring other big hard men down. And as the reggae musician Jimmy Cliff reminds us, the harder they come, the harder they fall.

It certainly takes it out of you. In a description of the changing room after a particularly gruelling game, Rick Reilly, writing for *Sports Illustrated*, shows just how spent and depleted the players were: 'One player sat slumped on a metal bench under a cold shower, too exhausted to take off his blood-caked uniform. Four were sprawled on the floor, IVs dripping into their arms. One of them tried to answer a reporter's questions, but no words would come out of his parched, chalky mouth. And that was the winning locker room.'[50]

All that impact, tackle after tackle after tackle, can leave you spent. You can see how hard the tackles are by looking at the language used to describe them. Tackles are 'crunching' or 'bone crunching', 'jaw dropping' or worse, jaw *breaking*. The *Urban Dictionary* includes a definition of the crunch tackle as 'A type of tackle, in the game of football, where the player that has the ball during play, gets hit hard as hell and knocked down in the same second or sooner.'[51]

Horse collars, spear tackles or not, there's no doubting that both American football and rugby are hard games, and you need to be fit and strong to play either of them. And Raymond is both of those. As

I mentioned in my preface to this very book, when I first met him, I remember him shaking my hand with such vigour that it actually hurt. This was when he was in his late sixties. I could imagine him crushing walnuts with his fingers when he was younger.

Raymond is strong and has been in sufficiently good shape to absorb impact after impact and take thousands of tackles over his long career. But the game is not just about physical impact, an ability to take the hits and dole them out in return; it's also about having an inner steel, a mental toughness that's as necessary as any helmet. When you meet Raymond, it's easy to reach for the cliched words 'gentle giant' – even if the handshakes have an iron grip – but on the pitch he was something different: tougher, steelier, able to absorb impact and pain. It might be labelled aggression, an ability to get in someone else's face. It was something he could turn on at will. Where does he find it in himself?

> I think everybody's got a certain level of aggression in them, and what I found that was more important than being able to turn on the aggression was to be able to turn off the aggression and to be able to be calm and normal and sensible and co-operative. For the most part of my life – I grew up a big guy and people would have an expectation that you would be aggressive and uncouth and demonstrative. But for the most part of my life I managed to control that and keep that in check.

That is, perhaps, as impactful a life lesson as any.

9.

A RAIDER AGAIN

The move back to Oakland didn't mean that Raymond was going to be playing right from the off.

When I was in the second year, Casper was still there, and by this time Tom Flores was the receiver coach and Madden was coach, so Casper and I were in competition. It was pretty obvious that there wasn't a whole lot of daylight between either of us in terms of who could play and who couldn't. I had a chance to re-establish myself as a real great player and the whole team knew it. Everybody knew it. That year a couple of receivers were hurt. At the time, Casper was still starting, but I was playing a lot, so somebody had the wild idea that we've got these two great players at tight end, and we've got a good player at wide receiver who's not yet become the great player that he could become, that is Cliff Branch, so we need to take advantage of these two players we got. So we did it experimentally in a couple of games, and we did so well that they said, why not? So we literally played the whole season with two tight ends and one wide receiver, and we had tremendous productivity out of that. We won lots of games and came very close to winning the division and going to the championship.

At the Colts, Raymond was misused and most certainly not properly utilised as a tight end who could really catch passes, even though people thought of him very highly indeed.

You have only to compare the scarce touchdowns for the Colts with the fourteen Raymond scored in his first two years with the Raiders. Tom Flores, Raiders head coach 1979–87, said in *Tales from the Oakland Raiders*, 'If you could sculpt a body for a tight end, Raymond Chester would be the model. If you were going to take a guy for speed, Raymond would be the guy. If you were going to take a guy for power, Raymond would be the guy.'[52]

In Oakland in 1979, they realised they were blessed with a pair of outstanding tight ends, and two fine pairs of hands, in Raymond and Dave Casper, so the coaches utilised an old tactic with an innovative new twist, being the two-tight-end offensive.

Raymond grabs a touchdown pass against Roosevelt Taylor of the San Francisco 49ers, 1970 (Photo: Ron Riesterer)

Other clubs used two tight ends in running situations. Over the course of his career, Raymond saw the tight end position redefined and played no little role in making that happen. It meant the disappearance of the sort of player who could easily block but who struggled to catch twenty-five passes, with a finesse player taking his place. Towards the end of his career, there was plentiful evidence of this change, this finesse, when it was not uncommon for a tight end such as Kellen Winslow – who played his entire career spanning ten years for the San Diego Chargers – to lead the league in receiving. Raymond recalls:

> When I started in the NFL, the tight end was a lineman. I loved blocking. I was consistently one of the better blockers on the team. I think what made me effective was my desire to excel and my aggressiveness. I was blessed with physical talent: speed, size, balance. But I considered myself a team player. I would be willing to catch fifty passes a season, or catch just fifteen passes and block every play. Whatever was needed to win, I was willing to do.

If the ball delivery was there, the tight end could use it. Ken 'The Snake' Stabler lit up the sky, completing 62 per cent of his passes. He distributed the ball evenly among his three primary receivers. Cliff Branch led the club with fifty-nine receptions while Raymond tallied fifty-eight and Casper had fifty-seven. Casper and Raymond would make NFL history by becoming the first pair of tight ends from the same team to make the Pro Bowl. Then Casper had a dispute with the Raiders, and they ended up trading both him and Ken Stabler midway through the 1980 season to the Houston Oilers.

Raymond enjoyed being one-half of a two-tight-end formation.

> That developed out of a situation…so I had three successful, no, super successful, years with the Raiders. My second year and now I have a whole camp and a chance to compete. There's Casper and myself, we had seven weeks in training

camp in which we could compete and vie for the starting job. So, it just so happens that Dave Casper was in contract negotiations with Al Davis, and the irony of it is that Al did the same to him as he did to me because he knew that he had an insurance policy and the insurance policy was me. He knew, to be honest, that I could play better than Casper anyhow. I was hungry to play, and I've got to think that Al Davis was playing us all like a fiddle as he knew our emotions and our anxieties, and it was amazing that he played us all as if we were marionettes.

But it was hard to know for sure. Al Davis was a very secretive man. He was once described as the CIA of American football; he kept his strategies hidden, like hiding a royal flush in a poker game. But he had the winning cards all right as his success rate proved.

Raymond believed that Davis, as well as his gifts for strategy:

Had a photostatic memory, and he demonstrated that not just to me but to many people, because if he was here now, he could tell you about every player that ever played for him or ever played for any team that we competed against. He could tell you where they were from, what their stats were, their school. Anyhow, he would not give in to Casper's demands because he didn't need him; he had me. So they got into a tremendous feud, but at the same time Stabler got into a feud with Al, so Casper and Stabler were holding out and Al traded them both to Houston – an old pro quarterback and an old pro tight end – they traded both of them with Jim and I on the benches. Then all of a sudden I got elevated to the first team. Jim Plunkett didn't immediately get elevated because they brought Dan Pastorini in from Houston, and he became the starting quarterback. But it wasn't long before Plunkett wound up being the starting quarterback and I was starting tight end.

So what makes a great tight end? The easiest way to find out is to ask one. Raymond reckons:

It's a movable thing, so you can have more than one, while some teams have none. The player called the tight end, he lines up for the most part on the end of the line next to the tackle. Now you can be on either side, and good tight ends can play on the right side or they can play on the left side. They have a set of plays that they run from the right side, and they can flip those over and play the same set of plays on the left side.

The thing is, it takes a whole different set of footwork to run that play on the left side than it does on the right side. Lots of players find it difficult to attack, to change from right tackle to left tackle – whoah that's a big, big, big change – right guard play switching to left guard play, a mighty big change. So the biggest thing the tight end has to have is versatility, then the things he's required to block on either side, running past routs on either side. So if you run a pass play on the right side and flip over to the other side, it's totally different footwork. So you need a pretty versatile guy – a guy who's required to catch, pass, to run, to block, to pass: the tight end is a versatile position, and I loved it because you got a chance to do most of the things that are to be done on the football field, offensively.

Raymond often found himself matched against some of the best linebackers in the business, the sort of hurtling bulks that took some stopping, and for some of them it was in the nature of a chore. They came at you and you stopped them. They came at you, then did so again, and you stopped them again. It was the sort of thing that could lead to repetitive strain injury on a grand scale! The most complete package Raymond ever faced was, in his opinion, Kansas City Chiefs star Bobby Bell. 'Bobby Bell was the smartest and toughest linebacker I ever played against. He had great knowledge of the game and he was just tough to move. Ted Hendricks was another one. We played together for a few years, too, but he was very quick and very strong. He was a difficult target to block.'

As he grew up near Baltimore, Raymond was able to watch one of the definitive tight ends in the game's history: John Mackey, the standard against which Raymond measured his own performance. 'John Mackey was always the guy. Every tight end wanted to be like him. He was the first tight end to really run with the ball after a catch.'

Tom Flores, who played for the Raiders from 1960–1 and again from 1963–6, was assistant coach for four years and then head coach from 1979–87. He has suggested that the Raiders always had a roster of good tight ends, from his playing days when the team featured the skills of Billy Cannon.

> Then, when I came back as assistant coach, we had Raymond Chester…chiseled and powerful. He had great speed for a big guy. He probably was one of the best man-on-man blockers because of his sheer strength…He could catch the ball and then run over or run right by people. So we took full advantage of his skills.
>
> We had to utilize Raymond because he was such a force. He made the Pro Bowl as a tight end with us all three of his early years, 1970–2, and again when he came back to us in 1979.[53]

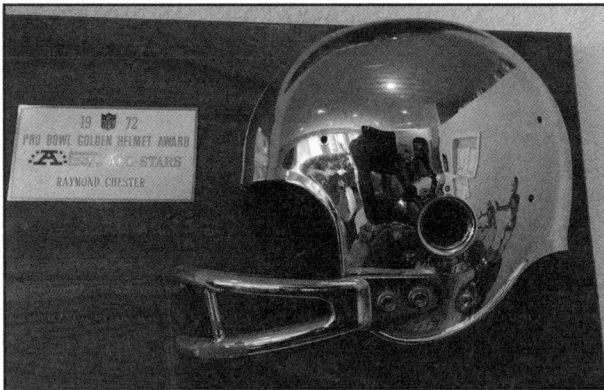

1972 Pro Bowl Golden Helmet award, Raymond Chester collection
(Photo: Jon Gower)

It was to be a very successful return, which included a proud footballing moment when he was awarded the Gorman award, which originated in 1967 and was renamed the Commitment to Excellence Award in 2022. As he stood on the pitch with his award in his hands, Raymond was joining a fine, impressive roster of previous winners, which included Daryle Lamonica, Jim Otto, Willie Brown, George Blanda, Marv Hubbard, Ken Stabler, Pete Banaszak, Mark van Eeghen and Dave Casper.

Tom Flores, in his *Tales from the Oakland Raiders*, explains that while the Gorman award-winning Raymond wasn't very fluid in his running style, being a trifle stiff when he took off, he was still a pretty tremendous specimen, able to overpower people at times in part because of this speed, a deceptive ability to be on an opponent fast, which was very much a surprise element as people simply weren't used to a tight end being able to put on a turn of speed. And in sport, the element of surprise is often a trump card.

Returning to the Raiders meant making new friends, of course. One of them was Morris Bradshaw, who played wide receiver. He had gone to Ohio State, under the legendary coach Woody Hayes, where the culture was very different to the Raiders.

Morris and Raymond had actually met via another sport altogether, as Morris recalls. 'We didn't meet on a football field. It was probably 1974 or 1975, which was my rookie year, the second year in the league. During the off-seasons we would play basketball, and that's where we met. I had no idea of the significance of it – he was just Raymond, had a van and he was driving!'

They had a lot of fun playing basketball even though their standard of play wasn't notably high. Morris suggests that, 'We all thought we were better than we were, and it was a fun time because you were in the van, you were traveling, playing the game and afterward having some beers, and then you go your separate ways until the next time you get together.'[54]

Being very much dependent on each other because of their positions on the field initially led to a friendship with Raymond, as Morris suggests, but then it widened and deepened.

The job, the playing, was something that we all had in common, but what I appreciated more than anything was getting to know someone in a context where football wasn't always the main thing. With Raymond being a little bit my senior, I was able to see what life might be like in the future with regard to relationships, family and playing, if you will.

Morris recalls how Raymond was the team leader, looking after younger players, and that the Raiders nurtured that kind of relationship at that time.

You made money – you made a good living – but you couldn't compare it with where it's at today, so we needed to rely upon one another. How do I buy a house? What do I need to do? And this was advice people readily gave you. I learned in my professional career that, you've heard the expression knowledge is power, and I also learned that in the case of some people, the withholding of knowledge is power. But the real power comes from sharing the knowledge.

Raymond recalls how competitiveness was left behind in the changing room, 'in all the things that Morris and I did together. Despite how competitive we had to be on the field, we didn't have a need to compete against each other off the field about anything.'

Debbie Bradshaw, Morris's wife, saw Raymond grow to be a member of the family. 'He was, is, a brother. He's family. I know if I needed anything he'd be the first call, and if he needed anything the same would be true. I have watched over the years a friendship become family.'[55]

Raymond ascribes much of the success in his career to being blessed with the presence, skill and, specifically, delivery of a phalanx of great quarterbacks, including 'The Snake'. The Oakland Raiders roster was very impressive, featuring players who each had distinctive skills they could readily display. 'Nobody threw long like Daryle Lamonica. Nobody was as good at reading defenses as

Ken Stabler. Nobody was as tough as Jim Plunkett. Nobody had the confidence of George Blanda. Nobody had the physical talent of Bert Jones.'

Ken 'The Snake' Stabler was the poster boy for Raiders' excess. He famously visited the Playboy mansion in LA during the week of the Super Bowl, having gone, in his own words, 'to share a few thoughts about football with some of the librarians there'.[56] His training regime involved a lot of bourbon, non-stop womanising, fast cars, even fast boats and, in truth, very few libraries. Had he perused the shelves, he might have seen a few titles by an author who would help thicken the aura of myth surrounding the Raiders, namely Hunter S. Thompson.

In 1973, *Rolling Stone* magazine had sent Thompson to embed with the AFC West team. Thompson was deep into gonzo journalism by this point, and as an avid football fan, he desperately wanted to chronicle a season with what was arguably the NFL's strangest team. Trouble was, Davis didn't entirely trust Thompson, and neither did the Raiders players, who the *Rolling Stone* writer allegedly plied with cocaine in order for them to open up (according to Robert Draper's history of the ground-breaking magazine, Thompson then tried to write the coke off as a business expense).

The journalist, often wired, encountered a man who seemed to be hooked up to the same electricity source, a compact man bedecked in a golf jacket who was agitatedly pacing at a lick along the length of the sidelines. Not recognising the increasingly famous writer, Davis asked Jack Smith, a sportswriter he knew from the *San Francisco Chronicle*, who the stranger was. Smith vouched for Thompson, explaining he had penned a good book about Vegas. That must have stopped Thompson in his tracks, for Smith neglected to mention the drug-fuelled debauchery of 1971's *Fear and Loathing in Las Vegas: A Savage Journey to the Heart of the American Dream*. Despite such literary credentials, Davis didn't like the look of the man and told Smith to swiftly evict him. 'Get the bastard out of here. I don't trust him.'[57]

Raymond was happy to be a cog again in the winning machine, under a winning coach. For he considers Madden to be 'probably one of the greatest communicators of our age' and harkens back to when the Raiders traded for him ahead of the 1978 season as an example of why.

Chester had started double-digit games at tight end in every year of his career up to that point but had taken a back seat to Casper in 1978. He was comfortable with it because of the way Madden handled the trade, and a year later Chester's role had increased again. He posted a career-high 712 yards in 1979.

Bob Chandler recalled Raymond's return to the Raiders in his book *Violent Sundays*, where he tells us that the team had a superb tight end in Raymond Chester 'who took over full time and really became a team leader. Raymond was the first-round draft choice who had been playing as many years as I had.' Over a dispute with the Raiders, Raymond had been traded to Baltimore, which he likened to a prison sentence. He played well enough to become All-Pro, and when his option was played out, Al brought him back to Oakland. Bob Chandler suggests that this was more than unusual. It was unheard of in the NFL. 'Once a guy was traded, he usually never returned to his old team. But Davis wrote his own rules and he believed that if one of his former players was still playing a fine game of football five years later, then, by God, he would just take him back.'58

Madden persuading Raymond to return to the Raiders hadn't been the easiest proposition to sell, as Raymond recalls. 'How do you get that kind of guy with that type of competitive nature, how do you get him to agree to come back and play second or third string on your team and everybody's happy about it? How do you do that? Because of the way it was communicated.'

Although back in his native Baltimore and succeeding the much-admired John Mackey, the ten-time All-Pro for the Colts, Chester was happy to return to the East Bay.

It was no secret, even to people in Baltimore, I liked Oakland. I've always felt inside as a Raider. I felt that I was born with the Raiders as far as my personal career was concerned and had nothing but good experiences with the team.

I accepted the [first] trade as being a part of life, although I admit I was confused and heartbroken. There were no fences to mend when I came back because I didn't allow a calculated decision on the Raiders' part to trade me in the first place to force me into reacting emotionally.

Once again, Chester proved to be a valuable, productive football player.

Raymond reckons that he wouldn't perhaps consider Madden the greatest strategist he ever came across but explains that the late coach's gift was the ability to get his message across to a locker room full of players. He thinks Madden communicated with a mixture of humour, candour and emotion, and understood that each and every player needed to be pushed a little differently. 'He was probably one of the greatest communicators of our age,' in Raymond's assessment. 'If you coach, the most important thing that you must be able to do is get what you want done across to your players.'

Raymond thinks those communication skills were very much apparent during Madden's thirty years as a legendary colour commentator as well, though Madden's coaching career wasn't too shabby, either. He posted a 103-32-7 regular-season record as the Raiders' head coach and won Super Bowl XI in January 1977.

When Raymond is asked about how Madden stacks up against all-time great coaches like Vince Lombardi and Bill Belichick, he stresses what a great communicator Madden was.

'The greatest gift that John Madden had was his ability to communicate,' Raymond suggests. 'We all got a taste of that. The world got a taste of that when he got into the booth and won all those Emmys communicating.'

Raymond was surprised when Madden retired from coaching at the age of forty-two. Tom Flores took over for Madden with the Raiders and won two Super Bowls, including one with Raymond Chester on the team. While Flores was succeeding in Oakland, Madden's broadcasting career took off.

Even though he knew Madden was a great communicator, Raymond was initially shocked that his former coach was interested in working as an analyst and that he was so good at it. In fact, he had another job in mind for Madden.

John Madden could've been a stand-up comedian. Ask anybody that knows him. Had he gone out and left football and become a stand-up comedian or left football and become a writer for a TV network writing comedy or something like that, I wouldn't have been surprised. But I don't think that anybody could say that they had any inkling or expectation that John would become as phenomenally great a commentator as he became.

Raymond thinks that when:

You think of a back-up quarterback; we had guys who could throw the ball and play the position. It wasn't just someone who could pick up the ball and just throw it. The Raiders created that: they allowed you to do that. They had to, because of all the personalities. They allowed you to be you, almost encouraged you to be you within a parameter. And the amazing thing for me was that at one o'clock on Sunday, everyone came together for one reason.

Everybody's goal was perfection in their craft. Nobody wanted to drop the ball. They wanted to learn how to catch a ball with one hand or in the other hand. Everybody was intent on being confident about beating one-on-one coverage. Everybody had to know what their adjustments were when we faced zone defenses or shift defenses, and even if you happened not to be one of the starting players on a Sunday or whenever there was going to be a time during the season when you were going to have to get on the field when you were expected by all of us to know your stuff, to know the rounds, the defenses or whatever. That's what fascinated me more than anything about the Raiders – you learned so much from so many different players and the whole goal was just to be better, the best. People don't know how good we were at understanding our craft, making sure everybody else on the team understood it, and so when a guy got a chance, he could execute it. There was that, and the brotherhood.

Dave Casper, a great tight end, we spent some years on the team together, right? We competed like hell, but we shared knowledge, we complimented each other, we came up with strategies together when it came to dealing with a specific team.

If anything is said about me, I would want it to be that I was a team player. That's the biggest and best thing someone could say about me in my career.

A prominent aspect of the modern game is working with the media, and Raymond has a long relationship buddying up onscreen with Mark Ibanez, the veteran sportscaster and director who had a forty-three-year career at KTVU. Indeed, Raymond was his first TV interviewee ever. Ibanez recalls:

I was so intimidated. I was twenty-three years old, had never been in an NFL locker room and this was a time of old suits, such as Ted Hendricks, John Matuszak, and they had just lost this heart-breaking game and I imagined them being in a horrible mood.

The place was clearing out and I had to get some interviews, and I'll never forget this – I asked Raymond for an interview, and he could tell I was jittery and kind of nervous. He said something to the effect of 'I can tell you're kind of new at this,' and this was tantamount to you saying let's fly to the moon. Professional athletes don't do this. He said, 'Sit down on that bench' – this was a time of benches, now it's all luxury – and made me comfortable. And you've got to remember, Raymond was built like an Adonis, an amazing physical stature, just like ripped, and would be very intimidating if he was behaving differently, being grouchy or mean, but he really made me feel at ease and comfortable. We struck up a friendship. When you walk into a professional athlete's locker room, that's their domain, you're a visitor there, and you have to have some areas that you can be in what I call a friendly oasis, a safe harbor.

We were friends right through his playing career, and afterward, when we started to do the Raiders podcast, when I was asked who I wanted as a partner, I immediately thought of him. I thought he was emblematic of what the Raiders stood for. He was a classy representative of the organization. I knew we had a bond that could translate to viewers and could make us both comfortable. You don't want to be on the air with somebody … Dwight Hicks, you know … nicest, smart dude, but you turn on that red light on the camera, you could see it in his eyes, he froze like a deer. I tried everything I could to relax him. You want to have that rapport. I thought Raymond was a big name; any Raider fan would know who he was, or they weren't really a Raider fan, and I also wanted to be on air with someone who would make me look good too! That's how I chose him, and there was no pushback from the producers as they gave me autonomy to pick who I wanted. Every year they'd say, 'Do you still want Raymond?' And I'd say, 'Yep!'

As a kid, growing up, I was a fan, season ticket holder to the Raiders. I was attracted to that skull and crossbones because as a kid I always liked pirates. And I remember as a fan that I was really ticked off that Raymond was no longer on the Raiders. A lot of Raiders fans were upset by that move because he was a prototypical Raider-type player – tough, gritty, almost larger than life, and I don't mean this in a pejorative way, but someone you don't want to mess with. Totally macho, outliers – not your crew-cut, goodie-two-shoes. I think of Johnny Knight as being the all-American, crew-cut football player, and I think the Raiders broke that mold. I think all the Raiders skated that fine line between that and obnoxious. You could walk into that Raiders locker room and feel a vibe of like anything goes.

One of the coolest things was the line between white and Black players seemed more blurred. Raymond was listening to the Rolling Stones, so for people our age, a lot of this revisiting of racial problems is frustrating. We'd already been there, put a fork in that.[59]

If you spend an evening with Mark Ibanez and Raymond Chester eating sliders and sipping whisky in a nice hotel in Napa, as I did, you'll be regaled with dozens of stories about the game. But what you'll also see is the chemistry between the sportscaster and the sports player, a ready warmth that easily communicated itself to TV viewers when they conducted the post mortems after a game. The bond between them is easy to see, and you feel, given the chance, they could talk about football and its intricacies until the cock crows.

10.

WINNING THE CHAMPIONSHIP: THE SUPER BOWL XV

Raymond has played in some big games, monster games, and in the Super Bowl, testing times when the pressure is ratcheted up and the tension turns tightly like a tourniquet. Some might sleep deeply, while others might calm themselves by listening to music. Some might withdraw into themselves and become as silent as Trappist monks, while others might jabber endlessly because of nerves or become tetchy to the point of violence.

Bob Chandler remembers in his book *Violent Sundays* many such coping strategies, although some of them sound like not-coping.

Mark van Eeghen, a great fullback for the Raiders, never felt he was ready until he threw up repeatedly. Raymond Chester, an All-Pro tight end, would engulf himself in music for two hours before the game. Dave Casper was the greatest, though. He had a nonchalant act where he would pretend he didn't care about anything. He'd sing, dance, joke around or sleep. I believed that inside he must have been churning because nobody could have been that good on the field and that relaxed beforehand.[60]

Some players had rituals involving the clothes they wore. Fred Biletnikoff would cut his jersey sleeves so that they would billow and hang loose, even when he was fined for doing so. It was all part of his pre-game preparedness, of getting himself into the zone.

So how much tension does Raymond feel before such games, indeed before any game?

> Oh. Every game. You know, the way in which a person handles tension and pressure is pretty unique to that person. I never had that sort of issue with it where I was vomiting or unable to sleep, but I'm sure there are other idiosyncrasies. But it was very common for guys to vomit or be unable to eat or be unable to sleep, but it depends on the guy how they really handle it because it's tremendous pressure. The reality of it is you'll have fifty to eighty thousand people on the stands scrutinizing every move you make, and you're going to have TV and radio and reporters chronicling every move you make, and then two million people sitting at home listening to the commentary on the radio or television. So if you allow it to put you under pressure, it will.

And if tensions run high in any game, then amplify and heighten according to the scale and importance of the occasion, then some games are up there in the clouds that swirl around Everest. The Super Bowl match-offs are not only pinnacles of the NFL calendar but also on the calendar for many Americans who, for the rest of the year, don't pay that much attention to football. Raymond puts it simply.

> The Super Bowl is the pinnacle of the game of American football, and many would say it's the pinnacle of American professional sport, period. It's certainly the biggest event

from the standpoint of attendance, television ratings and the international recognition of something that is uniquely American. Like any other championship, of soccer or baseball or basketball or hockey, to reach that level and to win at that level takes a combination of talent, obviously, but being lucky as I don't know what, staying healthy, you know everything has to fall in place in order to do that. Great players, fantastic players, great teams in terms of the year in terms of win and loss never make it to the Super Bowl, let alone win it. So many great players who have played for years and got all sorts of accolades never get to play in the Super Bowl, to win the big one, as they say. In games like that I've always managed to do well.

John Madden's last year as head coach of the Raiders was in 1978. The following year, Tom Flores was promoted from receivers' coach, ushering in a quiet, stoic, calm style after the showy bluster of Madden. Under the aegis of Flores, Raymond made the Pro Bowl again, catching fifty-eight passes for 712 yards and eight touchdowns. Then Raymond was an important part of the 1980 Super Bowl team, which ran to the glory that year, allowing Raymond to savour the taste of winning the trophy in his second-to-last year in the game. As he told Raiders historian Jerry Knaak, he was absolutely thrilled and honoured to be a part of that.

> So many times I'd been a bridesmaid. I'd played six or seven times in the playoffs – been in Oakland and we'd lose to Baltimore; they then go on to win the Super Bowl. Then I'm in Baltimore and they lose to Oakland, and they go on to the Super Bowl and win. Lose to Pittsburgh and they go on to win, so bridesmaid and never the bride...So this time it was a chance to not only go to the playoffs but go all the way to the Super Bowl.[61]

That 1980 team was the first wildcard team to ever win a Super Bowl, but the route through the playoffs was not without its real challenges. The Raiders were making their third Super Bowl appearance after posting an 11–5 regular-season record but losing a tiebreaker to the AFC West Division winner, the San Diego Chargers. Oakland then advanced to the Super Bowl with playoff victories over the Houston Oilers, Cleveland Browns and San Diego. The Eagles were making their first Super Bowl appearance after posting a 12–4 regular-season record and post-season victories over the Minnesota Vikings and the Dallas Cowboys.

Raymond traces the challenging path to the final. 'The Houston Oilers, we looked at them face to face, Stabler and Jack Tatum, very interesting.' The following week, the Raiders faced the Cleveland Browns in sub-zero temperatures as the wind whipped in over Lake Erie. Fortuitously, Mike Davis made the interception for the ages to secure that victory. Raymond recalls how they called him 'The Six Million Dollar Man' because should you work out what that play meant to the fans and the franchise, it certainly had to be worth at least six million dollars. Raymond recalls how Davis had tremendous speed and was a tremendous competitor and cover guy, but noted also that he had that disease, the defensive back disease that means you can't catch. 'There's a reason why you have great players like that on defense,' he told Jerry Knaak. 'If they could catch, they could have been a wide receiver but there are so many defensive backs who don't develop that skill, to be able to pluck the ball out of the air. But lo and behold, Mike makes that catch that catapults us on to San Diego and then on to the Super Bowl.'[62]

Raymond's longest reception in the San Diego game came early on, a sixty-five-yard touchdown that came off a deflection which gave the Raiders a 7–0 lead against one of the most high-powered offenses to ever take the field. That catch and the presence of mind in the moment that led to Raymond racing down the field really boosted the team:

> I've had the ball bounce the wrong way so many times, and then, boy, one time in your career it bounces the right way. That was cool; I had the position and the presence of mind to catch it but that's not the point. The point is that

at thirty-four years of age, I ran all of their defensive backs. So, everyone who wants to give me a hard time about the ball bouncing favorably, I'll agree with that, but it didn't have anything to do with my running around their backs. But what a game! That has to be one of the most fantastic games I ever played in, and that's not because of the long touchdown catch from me but because our team made some of the greatest plays. Some of the defensive work was unreal, and then there were six minutes' sustained drive, and they knew exactly what we were going to do, exactly where we were going to run it, and we just stuffed it down their throats for six minutes to close that game out. If you want to look at a game and see a total team effort, there it was. Hats off to our defensive backs because they had to play against what was at the time one of the most deadly offensive passing arsenals in the history of the league. That game was like the Super Bowl as far as I'm concerned. If the Raiders were ever magnificent, offensively and defensively, it was exemplified in that game.

Courtesy of such calculations made at speed, Raymond would reach a pinnacle of his career. He may still pinch himself…for in 1980, Raymond became a Super Bowl champion when the Raiders defeated the Philadelphia Eagles in Super Bowl XV (27–10). The pressure must have been enormous…

There will be those who fold under pressure, buckle and maybe lose the game for the team. So you have to deal with that sometimes…

Many times those same people have been instrumental in getting you to that point, to that big game. And then there are times when, no matter how good you are and how steely you are, you make mistakes. You fumble a ball, you drop a ball or whatever, and the trick is not to let that define who you are. The blessing is that, if you've been in a situation like that, we realize that we wouldn't have gotten to this position were it not for a particular player's contribution, and this is just one play that he wasn't able to make, a throw he missed, or a ball he dropped. So the general attitude from most of the players who understand that is to make it clear that we're not holding him responsible and that we understand it can happen to anybody.

Having said that, the things that are unacceptable are not fully knowing what you're supposed to do, fully knowing your job, not knowing the play, mental errors and whatever. Unacceptable. If that happens to you during the game, it's just lack of preparation, not taking it seriously and you're going to get a lot of dirty looks if you don't know your plays. Or you're not following the rules. We make physical mistakes; we all make them. We're human, after all, but there's very little tolerance for mental mistakes at that level. You don't forget your plays. You don't do stupid stuff. And if you do, man, you're going to get scrutinized and you're going to get criticized.

How quickly you think is key. It's a three-dimensional chess game with players moving around very, very quickly, and you've got the map of all the various plays in your head. And reflexes are crucial…What I've found is that the more you study, the better your doggone reflexes are. The more familiar you are with the material, the more confident you are and the better your reflexes are and the fewer mistakes you're going to make.

Now there are some guys – and you see this a lot – who are so gifted in terms of their athleticism, they're fast and they're big and strong, that they can compensate with their God-gifted skills for any mental mistakes that they make. Not so with most guys – there has to be a balance between knowing what you're doing, knowing what the adjustments are and the confidence that goes along with knowing the formula, knowing what you have to do and what not to do, knowing where we're going in a game. There's no substitute for that sort of confidence. Lots of times people compensate for it by being cocky and brash, but when it comes to the crunch, in the really critical situations, it's not there when you want it.

Bob Chandler recalls the excitement and colour of big games and Super Bowls.

We went down to San Diego to play the Chargers, and the whole city of San Diego went bananas. There were huge parades, and the day before the game was consecrated in holy tones as 'Charger Day'. The city was acting as if their team had already won the championship. Super Bowl Fever had overtaken the place. All of this hoop-de-dah really fired us up. Our tight end, Raymond Chester, ran around getting everybody fired up before the game. Incredibly, Raymond had never done this before, and we were all touched by seeing how much winning this game and putting our total effort meant to him.[63]

Motivation came easily to Raymond, who puts much of that down to growing up in a big family and to his family in particular.

It comes from being in a big family and seeing what my parents achieved – my mom with ten kids, she went to school, finished high school, went to college, graduated, got to grad school and came out with a doctorate. My sister working like I don't know what and then going to college to study music seriously, voice and singing opera and then graduating from John Hopkins, and my other sisters – Blanche, Angela, Davidia – all having masters and double masters. That was kinda in the family, and in a large family you always look out for your brothers and sisters, watching this or teaching that, so it was pretty natural. And then there were so many people in the Raiders who helped me through things and helped me understand certain aspects and techniques. By the time of, say, the eleventh year, that's who I was: I was a captain of the team. When I was with the Colts, I was designated a captain. There were at least a dozen on that team for whom I was their guy. They tuned into me and I tuned into the coaches. And that's how it was on every team. Coaches are sometimes over-rated. What they don't understand in many instances is this. So, you have to identify the guys on your team that can speak the same language, and if you're a smart coach, you can identify those guys and get them to share information on their behalf. I might have to go to some guy and say, 'Look, coach is unhappy; he thinks we're dogging it.' So you're delivering the message to five or six guys, and you multiply that by five, and the message is getting out there.

Helped by Raymond's motivational energy, the Raiders had beaten the Chargers on 'Charger Day', and the Super Bowl followed. Al Davis encouraged the players to bring their families with them to New Orleans for the big occasion and was happy to pay for all that.

So the Raiders found themselves playing the Philadelphia Eagles, who were worked almost to the point of exhaustion by their coach Dick Vermeil, while his counterpart Tom Flores kept the Raiders' training to a practice once a day. He was keeping energy in reserve.

As was by now traditional, Super Bowl XV was a game between the AFC champion Oakland Raiders and the National Football Conference (NFC) champion Philadelphia Eagles AND played in front of a gigantic TV audience. It would decide which side would be the NFL champion for the 1980 season. In this Super Bowl face-off, the Raiders became the first wildcard playoff team to win a Super Bowl.

The game was played at the Louisiana Superdome in New Orleans, Louisiana, on January 25, 1981, five days after the Iran hostage crisis ended. The game was thus held under patriotic fervour, as the pre-game ceremonies honoured the end of the crisis.

Aided by two touchdown passes from quarterback Jim Plunkett, the Raiders jumped out to a 14–0 lead in the first quarter of Super Bowl XV, from which the Eagles never recovered. Oakland linebacker Rod Martin intercepted Philadelphia quarterback Ron Jaworski three times for a Super Bowl record. Plunkett was named the Super Bowl MVP after completing thirteen of twenty-one passes for 261 yards and three touchdowns while also rushing for nine yards. Plunkett was also the second Heisman Trophy winner to be named Super Bowl MVP after Roger Staubach in Super Bowl VI. It was all a solid vindication of Al Davis's hang-loose approach before the sport's biggest annual audience.

The Raiders could run everything from their base formation, matching up all over the field without having to substitute. Raymond suggests:

> It's something that can be exploited today, but it isn't. We knew all the positions, all of the routes you could run, all the pass protections, and we were using the guys who had the most experience. So if I'm running up and down the field as tight end, one of the things I have the opportunity to do is really read and see the people playing against me. I can set them up for the time when I look like I'm going to make the same route but then break it a different way. So you have time to wear guys down and understand exactly what their idiosyncrasies are. That's the advantage of keeping the same battery.

There was arithmetic in play as well.

> We used to figure that we were going to have sixty-plus plays of offensive football between our running backs, you know, fullback, halfback, tight ends and two wide receivers. We figured we had to divide the number of touches that each guy got according to their ability to break plays and make plays. So we're going to get eight to twelve touches to Fred Biletnikoff or Cliff Branch, give the tight end six to eight touches and so on. And that would give you about sixty-five plays, which is what you're going to get. That was our scripting. I'm going to give the ball to Raymond six

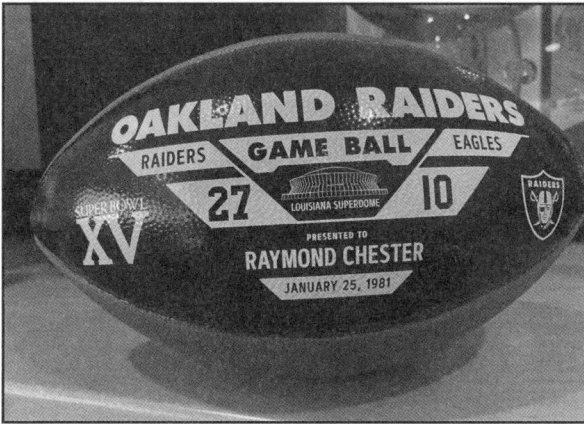

Super Bowl XV game ball,
Raymond Chester collection (Photo: Jon Gower)

to eight times in this game. I'm going to get the ball to Cliff twelve times. I'm going to give the ball to Freddie ten or twelve times. I'm going to give Kenny King fifteen to eighteen catches or carries, and that was the way we divided the game up.

It all comes down to the maths. Dividing sixty or so plays into individual efforts. Sixty million fans or so watching on TV. The pomp and glamour of the occasion. The fans trying to shout the roof off the Superdome. Bob Chandler suggested that for most of the guys out there on the field, 'it felt like the Kentucky Derby, the Indy Five Hundred and the heavyweight title all rolled into one'.[64]

When they got back home, the city of Oakland laid on a parade, with thousands of people standing in pelting rain to salute their heroes. Each player travelled in a vintage car while Al Davis gave everybody a special Super Bowl ring that had some thirty-two diamond chips around two large diamonds in the middle, all set suitably in silver and black to match the team's colours. The player's name, position, AFC Championship Game score and Super Bowl score were all duly engraved onto Davis's lavish gift. They didn't find out what they had cost but were later given to understand

Super Bowl XV ring (Photo: Cards84664 / used under CC BY-SA 4.0, https://creativecommons.org/licenses/by-sa/4.0/)

that they were evaluated for insurance purposes at $20,000. It is little wonder that Raymond wears his with pride. But only on very special occasions. Never when gardening.

After the Super Bowl, a group of the players was selected to take part in ABC's Super Teams, ten men who would represent the Raiders in the games against the Eagles and baseball teams such as the Kansas City Royals and the Philadelphia Phillies. So Raymond took his place alongside John Matuszak, Ted Hendricks, Mike Davis, Kenny King, Ray Guy, Rod Martin, Jim Plunkett, Bob Chandler and Lester Hayes, who all travelled first class to Hawaii to take part in events that included swimming, track relay and the obstacle course, which involved scaling an eleven-foot wall and climbing over monkey bars. Then there was the high jump, two hurdle races, a water jump and a final sprint for the finish line.

This being Hawaii, there had to be water sports too, so some of the games involved an outrigger canoe race where a slim boat had to be manoeuvred around a buoy, which was especially difficult considering a crew of seven big men had to fit in the slender native craft.

It was a televised event called the Superstar Competition. Raymond described it:

So basically, what it takes is three or four of the major sports events – in this case baseball and football – and they create a competition made for television. This one was in Hawaii, selecting eight of the players who were going to compete in various events such as swimming and canoeing, tug-of-war. The Raiders versus Philadelphia in the Pacific, under the sun. Sounds idyllic…

The tug-of-war thing fell apart because they cheated us, even those who were supposedly refereeing us. We clearly pulled them past the marker that we had, then they declared it a draw, and then we were disqualified. It was all totally unsportsmanlike. They had a grudge because we had beaten them in the Super Bowl: I'd have had a grudge too.

Raymond had long been proficient in a range of sports, so didn't find Hawaii too testing, not least because the competitions depended on teamwork more than individual performance.

Even with the individual accomplishments I had to my name, I was always a better team player. That was the difference between the Eagles and us at the time: we were a team. If it meant me sitting down and letting Matuszak take my spot or me having to swim the first leg on the swimming relay as opposed to swimming anchor, then that's what we did. I knew I was fairly decent in the 100-yard dash, that is for a big guy, but no way I could run like Cliff Branch. But I knew if they gave me a lead, I could run the third leg, which isn't popular, but I could run the hell out of it and hold my own. Then give the baton to Cliff Branch, and it's over. Nobody can run as fast as him, literally, in the world. And then we had Bobby Chandler left to run, and Bobby wasn't that fast, but he was as tough as you-know-what and guts like I don't know what, and we had Kenny King. You had to be really, really good to beat us.

The last event on the roster was the tug-of-war, where the Raiders were at a disadvantage as their team collectively weighed 150 pounds less than the Eagles. The teams took their places under the watchful eye of Bob Cousy, of Boston Celtics fame, who refereed the tug of a rope that sported a red flag in the middle to show which side had the upper hand. But when the whistle blew in the Raiders' favour, the other side went ballistic, while Ted Hendricks, the Raiders captain for the occasion, confirmed to his fellow teammates that they had won. But there was so much protest that it had to be staged again, which led to a stand-off, with teams refusing to do it again amidst threats of forfeiture.

When it came to big games, or even televised canoe races in Hawaii, Raymond underlines the essential role of readiness.

Getting ready, meticulously and thoroughly, mentally and physically, is key. I don't think there's any substitute for preparation in sport. No substitute. I don't care how good you are physically as an athlete; if you're in a situation and you're not prepared for it, you don't know what to do. It might be 40:60 that you do the right thing, but I wouldn't count on it, and I wouldn't want to count on it in the crunch, when you're competing against opponents of equal or even better physical talent than you. At that level, everybody out there can play. Everybody on that field can run. And they're tough. There's no way you can be out there unless you are. So if you're going to depend entirely on physical skills, it's 50:50 evens that you're going to win any personal contest in the overall battle.

Think about it. The game is a big game, and the team is trying to accomplish goals, but there are games within the game in which some players are trying to individually win more than they lose. So let's look at X versus Y. Just because someone is, say, twenty-five pounds heavier and three inches taller or whatever, he's just going to have his way with the other player isn't he? That's the mistake that so many people make. Because there is a balance between technique and situational awareness and physical skill and mental capacity and above all the ability to stay focussed.

You see it all the time; you see guys lose focus when they make mistakes, when they drop a ball or fumble a ball or they miss a kick and they get all tore up. How long does it take them to get back in the zone, to focus again?

One of the things that happens in today's game – especially with the younger players – in every sport is they become over jubilant about doing something well, going overboard in celebration after doing something well that is supposed to be a part of their job. You're a pro, you're out there, you're getting paid. Yet they do something well, and then all of a sudden they're jumping up and down and they're dancing...that is as much of a distraction as the guy with his head in his hands who's sulking because he dropped the ball or missed a kick. What does it take to go from jubilance to focus? Or from being distraught to being focussed? You can't get overexcited because you do something well. Maybe a second where you think, 'wow', but getting all the other guys involved in the jubilance when the game isn't even over, well, you've got plenty of time to do that when the game is over.

When I see that, I think it's terrible. It's a major, major, major problem in sports today. Some players can refocus quickly and be back on the ball a lot quicker than others, and believe me, that's one of the signs of whether someone is a great player or not. How quickly he refocuses physically, mentally and emotionally.

One of the things you learn very, very early on as an athlete – if you perform at any significant level, at college, the pros or whatever – is how to tune out the crowd. You just learn that they're there, but they're not there at the same time. What you see is your teammates and the opposite teams, and then when something happens which is positive, then, you flip the switch. You hear the adulation from the crowd and it encourages you. But when something not so good happens, you hit the same switch and you tune it out. So you try to use the crowd to incite your team and excite you or motivate you or even to piss you off to the point where you want to play better.

In order to do your best and play your best, you need a good level of concentration, of focus. The team that sustains that over the longest period of time is usually the team that wins. If they can get most of their guys to concentrate most of the time and the talent level is there, they usually win.

INTERLUDE:

SPEED

Noun.
Definition. Swiftness or rate of performance or action.

'Football is a speed game,' said Coach Kevin Bullis at Division III powerhouse Wisconsin Whitewater.
(*Washington Post*, September 2021)[65]

The NFL American has its speedy players galore, and some of them are so fast that they beg the question: are they actually faster than track and field athletes? Raymond, who had been a track athlete in his college days, had speed on his side as a player. He could run the 100-yard dash in 9.8 seconds and then sprint the forty-yard dash in 4.45 seconds. That's a speed of 20.87 miles per hour. He wasn't the fastest in the game, but he was far, far from being the slowest.

For a little bit of context, each and every year, the NFL tracks the fastest players each game. A total of thirty-six NFL players ran faster than 21 mph during the 2022 regular season, but only Parris

Campbell and Kenneth Walker surpassed the 22-mph threshold. Campbell's 22.11-mph speed ranks as the fifth-fastest top speed by a ball-carrier during an NFL season since 2016.

Speed is one of the principal reasons why the talented Welsh rugby winger Louis Rees-Zammit was selected by the NFL as a member of its International Player Pathway. It was Welsh rugby's loss and the NFL's gain. When the Welsh wing Louis Rees-Zammit announced he was leaving the national squad to try his hand at NFL football, you could hear a deep collective sigh of disappointment. After all, here was a mercurial winger who had quickly won the respect of fans and run rings around opponents on the pitch to boot, courtesy of his astonishing acceleration. The already brilliant star decided to put his rugby career on hold to chase his 'dream' of playing American football. 'I'm excited, I can't wait to see the difference. I get that question all the time; what is harder hitting, rugby or American football? We'll soon find out,' he said. 'It's going to be fun. I've played a contact sport since I was twelve. That's bone on bone but we'll see what it's like when we come to pads.'[66]

The NFL's International Player Pathway has been in place since 2017, allowing select divisions to be allocated players. In September 2023, it announced that the NFL was increasing opportunities for international players that would see practice squads expanded to seventeen players if a qualifying player was included. Tampa Bay Buccaneers owner and chair of the NFL international committee Joel Glazer said at the time: 'The opportunity for all thirty-two clubs to utilise an additional practice squad roster spot for an international player is a significant step forward in helping to identify, develop and enable more exciting talent from around the world to play in the NFL.'[67]

Rees-Zammit explained, 'I'm trying to learn as much as I can and trying to bring what I've got already in rugby to the American football side of it, and give it my all.'[68]

Rees-Zammit signed for the defending Super Bowl champions Kansas City Chiefs and appeared to be making a good impression in training. But sadly, he didn't make it into the squad.

That said, Louis Rees-Zammit is fast. The Welsh TV broadcaster S4C put their own speedometer on him in a game, showing Rees-Zammit reached a top speed of 24 mph, or 10.73 metres per second (m/s). This easily beat one of his own previous top speeds when he'd been clocked at 23.48 mph in a game for the English side Gloucester against Saracens.

In a totally different context, that running speed is half that of a mountain lion or puma when it's really running. Although you might run even faster if you had a puma coming after you!

Louis Rees-Zammit had properly shone in rugby, including some real moments of acceleration. One of the most memorable came in a home game in Cardiff's Principality Stadium when the young winger received the ball pretty much at one end of the pitch, inside his own ten-metre line, chipped the ball in front of him and successfully gave chase to it, beating his opponents who had a twenty-metre start on him.

It's uncommon to hit such speeds during a match as it's easier to concentrate in the controlled environment of the training ground, but players such as Rees-Zammit can step on the gas. Another player who did so was the New Zealand winger Rieko Ioane, who ran at 10.69 m/s (23.92 mph) when making a successful try-saving rapid chase and downing tackle against old rivals Australia.

Meanwhile, American Carlin Isles carries the tag of rugby's fastest man. He has previously recorded a top speed of 11.5 m/s (25.7 mph) and has a 100-metre PB of 10.15 seconds.

So, NFL athletes are some of the best in the world, but Rees-Zammit's pace makes him a contender, with quarterback Patrick Mahomes stating recently that the twenty-three-year-old's speed 'is real'.

Hopefully, Rees-Zammit will have much more success than another Welsh player, Paul Thorburn. In 1987, the Los Angeles Rams faced off with the Denver Broncos in a pre-season game at Wembley Stadium. While it was a 'friendly' in truth, it was marketed as the 'American Bowl' to attract more attention. It was only the second time that NFL teams had met in London (1986 had seen the Chicago Bears face the Dallas Cowboys).

In London's Wembley Stadium, Wales and Neath full-back Paul Thorburn was invited to suit up and play. The move was a mixture of publicity stunt and a more serious part of the international scouting process. Had the Neath man impressed, there was the potential of his having a serious chance of further try-outs for the LA Rams. But unfortunately for Thorburn, his initial kick-off was so unimpressive he played no further part in the match at all, and his career was summarily curtailed. Luckily, Thorburn is remembered for other kicks, as he was a prolific long-distance goal kicker. He holds the record for the longest successful kick in an international test match, with a penalty kick measuring exactly seventy yards, eight and a half inches (64.2 metres) against Scotland.

PART FOUR:

LIFE AFTER NFL 1982-PRESENT

11.

THE INVADERS AND USFL

So what does a man do after an extra-long career in the NFL, racking up tens of thousands of hours training, putting in testing performance after testing performance, week after week, season after season? When the body has been pushed to its limits and then back again, over and over. Well, after a long career playing for the Raiders, then the Colts and then the Raiders again, Raymond had one more team left to play for. Just when his dynamic and very long National Football League career had drawn to a close, along came the USFL to give the former Oakland Raiders and Baltimore Colts tight end another life. The USFL wanted to set up as a rival league and not just share some of the limelight but, if possible, take a lot of it away for themselves.

One of the catalysts for establishing the new league was the departure of the Raiders for Los Angeles and the more spacious, and therefore more profitable, Los Angeles Coliseum before the beginning of the 1982 season. This was a move that would prove to be controversial and unpopular. Fans went ballistic. Businessman Ted Taube tapped into this discontent when he established the Oakland Invaders, with its deliberate poetic echoing of the Raiders in its name. The city of Oakland's mayor at the time, Lionel J. Wilson, was just one of those who felt that taking the Raiders south to Los Angeles left his city high and dry and that the creation of the Invaders would please fans left bereft. He also felt it in his bones that one day the Raiders would be back and, much more than that, back where they belonged.

Originally called the Bay Area Invaders, the team, under coach John Ralston, had a shaky start to their first season. They let the Birmingham Stallions run away with a game, were outshone by Denver Gold, proved too slow to match Los Angeles Express, were outshone by the Philadelphia Stars, robbed by the Tampa Bay Bandits and bombed out 7–31 against the Chicago Blitz. Luckily, the Invaders dug in deep and searched for a winning streak, managing to win five out of their final eight games to gain themselves the Pacific Division title and a place in the playoffs. In this, they were matched against the Michigan Panthers, who clawed their way to victory in front of a crowd of over sixty thousand fans in the Pontiac Silverdome. Raymond led the squad in that season's catches, racking up a total of no fewer than sixty-eight catches for 951 yards, far from a bad showing for someone who was now earning himself the moniker of steely veteran.

The following season was far from successful, more often a case of the Invaders being fully repelled. Their first game saw them scoring no points at all, losing 0–9, and they would only manage a total of

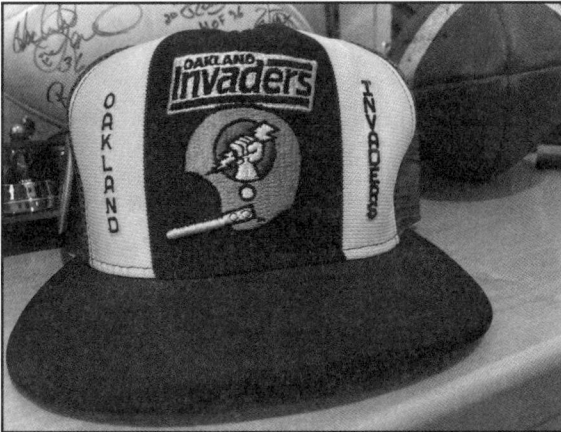

Oakland Invaders hat, Raymond Chester collection (Photo: Jon Gower)

eighty-two points in the first half of the year. It was getting to the point where they could count the points they amassed in a game on their fingers and, at its worst, the fingers of one hand. The augurs were not good. They tried a new coach, with Chuck Harris stepping into the breach in the fourth month of the year, and he managed to start turning things around, even though success proved elusive for another six weeks. Once they had found their collective mojo, they managed a run of seven successive wins, which acted as a balm to bruised collective pride. The Invaders regained a little respect, courtesy of doubling their tally of points in the second half of the year and a defensive line that held taut and tight whatever was being hurled at it.

It's not that Raymond's career in the NFL was dead – he had ample opportunities to continue his career with more than one team after being cut loose by the Raiders prior to the 1982 season. But the USFL's Oakland Invaders offered more.

Raymond claimed at the time that he could still play tight end with the best of them, and his performance levels backed him. This made him a key ingredient in the Invaders' embryonic team. But he also became the new club's assistant marketing director, selling season tickets and speaking at the Invaders' boosters club and thus mixing a marriage of duties not many men would be comfortable with. But this was a new career path, a business opportunity that really attracted Chester to the USFL's Oakland entry.

> I had an opportunity to play another year or two in the NFL as a back-up tight end or even a starter. But the Invaders offered the challenge of getting in on the ground floor and being an integral part of the organization.
>
> A lot of people were sad, disillusioned and shocked by my exodus from the Raiders, but I knew it was going to happen. I didn't feel bad. The big thing was I had my health. I was left with several options.

His desire for playing hadn't diminished, however. Chester couldn't wait for the opening of training camp in February and the inaugural USFL season.

'I haven't felt this excited about a season in ten to twelve years,' Raymond said at the time. 'It'll be a super-great feeling to be back in the Coliseum. I feel like a rookie. In a sense we are rookies. I was looking at our roster the other day and we have an average of about two and a half years' experience.'

It would be up to the skills, experience and, well, wiliness of a handful of veterans, like Chester, Cedrick Hardman and Delvin Williams, to provide a steadying influence on the younger players. Raymond also looked forward to proving to himself, and to a crowd, that his body could still be a devastating offensive weapon.

Raymond anticipated nothing but success for the USFL, and the league's signing of collegiate stars such as Tim Spencer, Craig James, Reggie Collier and Trumaine Johnson only served to fuel his optimism, while he didn't entirely discount the possibility of an eventual merger with the NFL, even though that was not the USFL's goal. It was, rather, setting up a big-league operation, with big-league commentators and pro football in the same calibre as the NFL. It was a rivalry of leagues much like that of teams playing within a league.

As the USFL's history shows us, Raymond, twelve-year NFL veteran, was soon one of the leading receivers in the United States Football League. At the age of thirty-five, he didn't seem to have lost pace or physicality. He amassed 100 or more yards on receptions in three games, which matched the number of 100-yard games he had during an NFL career, in which he made the Pro Bowl four times. When asked how long he could keep it up, he answered, 'I play a game at a time; every week I see how I feel. I haven't set any goal as far as how long I'll play. This could be my last year. I don't know.'

What he did get to know was that the USFL wanted his name and his body. Raymond said that he turned down several NFL teams after his release from the Raiders. But he found this offer too tempting to resist.

As they opened their first season, the Invaders seemed to be satisfying the appetites of fans who still longed for the return of their once-beloved Raiders, now based in Los Angeles. The club sold more than twenty-five thousand season tickets. But they averaged about ten thousand no-shows per game, as a team in its first year tried to engage with its fans in a way comparable with a team that was twenty-three years old. Indeed, the Oakland Raiders happened to have one of the best winning percentages in all of sports. It was always going to be a tall order.

The Raiders, after twelve seasons in Southern California, eventually moved back to their original city. Then, in 2020, the Raiders left Oakland again and moved to Las Vegas and the newly built Allegiant Stadium, which seats 65,000 and can hold up to 71,835 people.

As the Invaders' offensive captain, Raymond did his level best to help his teammates cure their on-the-field ills.

But the Invaders ultimately failed, as did the upstart league in which they played. Even though the team managed to reach the Championship Game, they had lost the enthusiasm of fans. To compound their misery, they narrowly lost that USFL Championship Game against the Baltimore Stars in Giants Stadium, 24–28. Attendances for other games had been dwindling. A paltry 12,740 dribbled through the turnstiles for the home game against Portland Breakers at the substantial Oakland-Alameda County Coliseum, making it impossible to make ends meet, even in a league which capped players' salaries in order to do so. Haemorrhaging money meant Taubman had to make a decision, and the wealthy businessman decided to pull out, leaving the Invaders in the red, thus having to suspend operations for the 1986 season. But the writing was on the wall for the league as a whole, and the Championship Game between the Invaders and the Stars was the last ever game in the USFL's history, as an anti-trust suit between the league and the more powerful NFL was lost, and they were awarded a mere three dollars, not even enough to buy a hot dog *and* garlic fries.

This sad visit to the graveyard of broken dreams offered a rare taste of failure for Raymond, who was still glad they gave it a go. Because he gave it his all, as is his wont. It's a hallmark of the guy. He doesn't do half-measures. In pretty much anything. It was time, though, to try a new course in life, and that was a golf course.

12.

A SMALL WHITE BALL

What next for Raymond? With the mayfly life of the Oakland Invaders slowly slipping into history, along with the very league in which they played, it was time to take stock, to find new purpose in a life which had revolved around keeping fit, fitting into the team and playing the game. It's no easy matter going solo, leaving life as a team sportsman, and especially so when you've been involved in a game for decades, as was true in Raymond's case. If you've been training pretty much every day and playing hard, pushing your body to the limit on a daily basis, then sitting around watching the grass grow isn't an option, or at least it shouldn't be. But when the brief life of the USFL was snuffed out and Raymond had to ponder his future, what was he to do? He had a brief time in real estate, doing exams and clinching deals and, like most other things in Raymond's life, he made a success of it. But there was something missing. What was it? What could he do that would offer a more rounded sense of satisfaction?

The answer came in the shape of a smaller ball than the one he'd been used to, in the game of golf. It gave him not only the challenges of learning a new sport but eventually gave him a new source of income, which suited him to a tee, if you pardon the pun. It was also a way of connecting with his younger self when golf had been a source of very hard-earned dollars.

When Raymond was entering his teenage years in Baltimore, twelve or thirteen years of age, he and his friends were forever looking for ways to make extra money. They would mow grass in the summer and shovel snow and clear the driveways in the winter, and in between seasons would run errands, do pretty much anything people in the neighbourhood needed to have done. By dint of their labours, they would get rewarded with a few quarters or dollars, always dropping far, far short of making their fortune. Raymond recalls:

> We'd go to the supermarkets and assist people with their bags, take them to their cars. And then someone said you can get a job at the golf course, which was miles away from us, and all you have to do is carry two bags for people, walk around on a nice golf course, which is like a park, and you carry a bag with clubs in them and they all have numbers on.

There would often be a long, cold trudge out to Woodholme Country Club in northwest Baltimore, which is right on the border of the county and city limits, so a long way from the inner city where Raymond lived. In memory, he measures the distance:

> It was, I bet you, twelve miles. When we got there, we didn't know what to do, so we stood around. One day, I'm standing there, and the caddy master comes over and says, 'You're a big strong kid; I need you to help Mr Johnson here.' I said okay even though I had no idea what to do. He said all I had to do was carry the bag, stay quiet, stay out of the way, keep up with them when they walk, and when they ask you for a club, just take the club out of the bag and give it to them.

Raymond recalls how they had to be really quiet and observant so that they could see where the little white ball went, whether it veered to the right or to the left, and then how they had to hustle down to find it. But, of course, they couldn't actually touch it, having to just stand there like a human fingerpost and inform the golfers of the location of the ball. And if they carried out the ball-spotting really well, found all the balls and kept up with the players as they went around the course, they'd probably be given two or three dollars. And if they got really adept at the task, they might graduate to carrying not one but two bags and then might make five or six dollars, just for walking around. Typically, then, these young people were earning between eighty-five cents and a dollar an hour for their labour, so Raymond calculated he could carry a couple of bags around for four hours and make five or six dollars! 'I knew nothing about golf before that, had no interest in playing. My interest was in making five or six bucks, easy. This was my first introduction to golf.'

He might put in a shift of four or five hours of walking around the course, that is, after walking to the club in the first place:

> Then we carried those around for four or five hours, got paid for that, and then, in the evenings, they had parties and dinners and whatever. If you really got to know people, after caddying you could go work in the kitchen, stand in line to go work in the kitchen after a day on the course. Washing dishes and washing pots, peeling potatoes, I would spend the whole day and night at the country club. By the time we finished cleaning up, it was two in the morning before we walked home again because even though we had some money, the buses stopped running at one a.m.

Despite all the long hours he had put in caddying, Raymond had never actually hit a golf ball until he moved to Oakland. 'I had come to play for the Raiders, and I lived in Alameda, where there were two golf courses, but I then bought a home in the Oakland Hills. I started to meet people and get invited to events.'

During the first such event, Raymond had to admit that, despite having been on a golf course many times, he hadn't actually ever handled a club. So here he was, a celebrity and an athlete who had to go out there and do his best to stay on the right side of humiliation:

> They choose you, and they're happy to have you in their competitive group, but you can't hit that ball. It goes all over the place. And these little fat guys who never did anything athletic in their lives, they can play golf; they can hit the ball. Everybody's trying to teach you how to hit it and telling you, 'It's easy, you just do this,' but when you do that, it makes solid contact but yet goes pretty much anywhere. The more they tell you how to do it, the worse it gets.

And it did get worse: 'My second experience of golf was playing in a tournament like that without having had any experience or any lessons or whatever and exposing myself to total humiliation. Total humiliation.'

It would have been enough to make most men sell their clubs. However, Raymond not only got back into the game but ended up running a golf course near Lake Chabot in Oakland and becoming a partner in another.

> There was an old African-American guy called Bob Johnson who was a sort of Satchel Paige of golf, Paige being a Black baseball pitcher. Johnson grew up with golf and became a skillful player, a prodigy, to the extent that he wanted to play in the tournaments and turn professional. He was good enough, but he happened to be Black, and in his day there was no opportunity for him to play golf. This was before the likes of Charlie Sifford – the first African American to play on the PGA Tour. So Johnson caddied, and he learned how to craft and adjust clubs and didn't get a chance to play a tournament until he was in his sixties.

Raymond recalls playing at one of these tournaments, and it was a horrible thing to watch. Then Bob Johnson introduced himself and said he was a golf instructor who admitted he couldn't take it anymore. He couldn't watch someone he considered to be one of the greatest athletes in this town, an awesome athlete, a Raider, a big strong guy, humiliate himself on the golf course anymore. He offered to teach him to play.

> Of course with golf, you're never quite there; you're always working to improve. And also there are so many variables. You can play wonderfully one day and horribly the next. Golf is as much a mental challenge as it is a physical challenge, and you have to get some kind of control over that thing we all have called ego. It will at some point humiliate or humble anyone who's played it. And that's the beauty of the game. It's you against the course and the elements, and then you against yourself. My dad had a saying, he'd say, 'Raymond, I want you to remember something. A lot of things will happen when you're playing a sport, and you're a good athlete, but remember you stay calm; you stay who you are. And remember that you're never as good as they say you are. But the contrast to that is you're never as bad as they say you are either!' I have tried for some seventy-odd years to remember that.

By this time, everybody wanted the pro-athletes and celebrities at their golf club. So, after Raymond had learned how to play a little, some of his teammates – Jack Tatum, George Atkinson and Daryle Lamonica – all started learning to play golf as well. As Raymond explains:

> We figured out that it was a great social event, and so I started playing with my teammates, such as George Blanda and Jim Otto – and we had so much fun drinking beer and playing golf and laughing at each other and teasing. Some would move the ball all over the place, and we would have

little bets…So we did that for many years, having breakfast together, then some rounds of golf, say thirty-six holes, and then we would go to the pub and drink a few pints. And we would joke saying, you know, it took us all this time to get smart enough to find a sport where we could hit something that doesn't hit back!

So how good did he get? Currently Raymond doesn't have a golf handicap. 'At best it was six, and there were maybe four times when I shot under par, two or three under, stuff like that. I guess my handicap now is fifteen, but I don't play a lot now.'
Raymond fully enjoyed the golf course and club at Chabot.

I'd learned at an early age that professional sports, especially in my era, wasn't a career; it was a very temporary job. I'd seen examples of people who had climbed pretty high, like Joe Louis who had made headlines and made money, and then come crashing down. It really was painful to see that because they were our heroes, Afro-American. You've got a few heroes like that: made a big name but blew their money. I had this thing in my head that if I ever made any money, I was not going to wind up being broke.

When Raymond took over the Chabot golf course, he had his work cut out for him. It had been open since 1937 and had deteriorated considerably as the city couldn't afford the necessary reinvestment. Raymond also had one fundamental issue to sort out. 'I knew nothing about the golf business, so I brought in the golf pro. And it worked. I ran that golf course from 1987 until 2007, twenty years plus. Good years.'
They were not years without their challenges.

Someone once told me this is one of the most demanding things you'll do, Raymond, and I said what? And he said you've got thousands of people coming in, and you've got this big farm and all that can have an impact – the agri-economy, the weather, rain, drought, or pests and pestilence. Then you've got the restaurant to run from sunup to sundown, and you're also running a retail store with all the inventory and items to keep track of, the back-of-the-house operation. And all of this was going on at the height of the Tiger Woods phenomenon, when everyone wanted a piece of golf, so it was like gaining a PhD in business management, with politics and retailing in the mix. It's why I don't have any hair!

Some of the natural problems arrived with claws on.

There might be a mountain lion on the golf course, or pinworms, which can infiltrate the surfaces of your putting greens, or fungus on the greens. Normally, if you see a mountain lion, it's by accident because they're usually so stealthy, so it's because you've come near to a recent kill they've hidden off somewhere in the bushes. In general, they want to go their way and have nothing to do with us, and they like night time or early mornings and evenings. It was always interesting when someone came in having spotted a mountain lion or rattlesnakes – we had a lot of rattlesnakes and we had coyotes as well.

Raymond likes to point out that he retired not once, not twice but three times. He left the NFL, he left the USFL and eventually left the tee in what constituted a second career in golf management. His time at Chabot, high in the hills above Oakland, had given him plenty of fresh challenges but, just as he'd had to finally hang up his football boots, it was time to put the club in the caddy for the last time and look for a more recreational way of spending his time. He would find it in fishing, a sport and pastime that would give him satisfaction as deep as some of the lakes and rivers he would visit all over America.

13.

GONE FISHING

Picture the scene. Two men are hitching trailers to their trucks in the pitch dark before stowing rods and tackle and all the supplies they need for a good day's fishing. It is still too early for the birds. It is still too early for the sun to burn some colour into the day.

Raymond's buddy for these expeditions is Dave Killingsworth, and they have been fishing together for so long that their joshing and joking and leg-pulling is set on automatic.

Raymond's first experience of fishing was with his grandfather, using just a line and a hook, with a sinker on the line, fishing by hand.

> We did that a lot when we were on these small skiffs or boats, fishing for striped bass, some hardhead and various types of saltwater fish. The first place where I got an orientation about fishing was with my dad in Golden Hill, Maryland, which is on the outskirts of Cambridge. It's where my grandfather's farm was, and my dad used to take me out on a little skiff without a motor on it or anything. And he had a long pole which he would use to push us

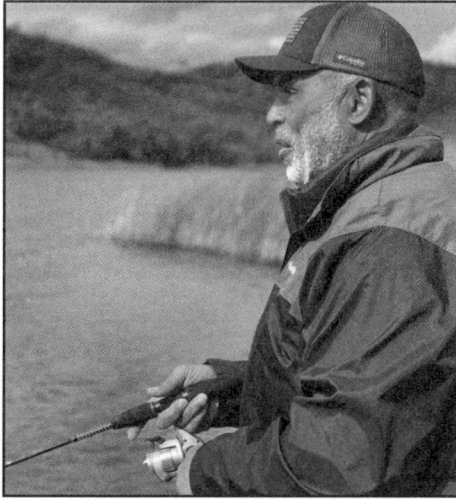

Gone fishing (Photo: Martha Hill)

through the water, and we'd catch crab, which we would then disassemble to use the parts as bait to catch perch, flounder and pogie, or Atlantic menhaden and striped bass.

Raymond has many favourite fishing spots in the States, depending on the time of year. 'There's no better place than Northern California – there's so much freshwater and a wealth of lakes and ponds. The bass and the trout and the pan fish – crappie and bluegill and perch – are just vibrant, and the fishing is as exciting as I don't know what.'

He travels widely to go fishing: as far as Alaska.

I love Alaska. You're camped out on the bank of a river and there are bears, no doubt about that, and even more dangerous are moose. In Alaska, and I think this is a fact, moose kill more people than black bears or brown bears. Alaska is the wilderness.

I do lots of lake fishing, mountain lakes and so on, but when you're in places like Delaware, Maryland, Mexico and California, it's often ocean fishing for everything from bluefish to marlin to tarpon. Some of them are big fish; the biggest I caught was a sturgeon, and I love sturgeon – one of my favorite things to fish. I once caught a 145-pound sturgeon in the Sacramento River in California that was over seven feet long, and I caught it on a twelve-pound test line. It had a marvelous flavor too.

Raymond, like so many fishermen, lives with the fact that there are increasingly fewer fish to be caught. 'Fewer salmon in Alaska, fewer sturgeon in San Francisco Bay. As a fisherman, there's cause for concern as fish stocks go down.'

Dave and Raymond are not exactly quiet fishermen: the perch can hear them coming. They banter wittily back and forth, and yet there *are* times of quiet and of contemplation. They both love nature. One time they were out in the boat on Lake Sonoma when they saw an osprey take a fish out of the water in the middle of the lake; it brought it up, and a bald eagle saw it and went for the fish. Challenged in this way by a much larger bird, the osprey let the fish go, the bigger bird then plunging into deep water even as it opened its huge wings like a cape around its prey.

As Dave explains: 'No one day is like the next. I've been fishing for sturgeon when a sea lion tried to steal it, so while the sturgeon is fighting me, he's in fact trying to get away from the sea lion. I've also caught a salmon and, all of a sudden, a big shark will come in and steal it – whack – like that.'[69]

Raymond certainly has instinctive skills when it comes to assessing fishing waters, pulling together a lot of knowledge, amassed over years. 'So much of what we do depends on the water and the elements. The temperature, time of year, smell, whether it's raining, depth, structure in the water, trees or rocks or sand, which baits are prominent, insect blooms – all these factors dictate what type of fish may be there and how to catch them.'

Betting is, for these two anglers, an entertaining part of the overall experience, as Dave explains: 'We bet on the first fish, the most fish, the biggest fish or the best variety or we'll put a premium on a certain species, and the length and girth and weight.'

Raymond hunting Canada geese,
Raymond Chester Collection (Artist: Calvin Grey)

Raymond also enjoys hunting. He once clubbed in with some friends to buy a hunting ranch in Eureka, California, where they shot geese, duck and pheasant. He would also take a gun to Tule Lake, a place packed with birds in winter when Tundra Swan, Northern Pintail, Cackling, Canada, Snow, Ross's and Greater White-fronted Geese all visit in their tens of thousands.

Raymond describes himself as a:

Handy man with a gun. I learned to shoot with my grandfather and my father on my grandfather's farm with a single-barrelled shotgun. I would go walk with them while they hunted as there was only one gun in the family, my grandfather's J.C. Higgins shotgun where the ejector on it didn't work, so every time you had one shot, you had to then break the gun down. My dad had a steel bolt he would drop down through the barrel and that steel bolt would punch the empty shell out, and then we'd load it again and carry on rabbit hunting.

There are aspects of fishing that appeal to Raymond beyond the companionship of fellow fishermen and the sport of the catch. He feels much closer to God out in nature.

That's part of the allure for me, the connection with God and nature and creation. Then the coordination and syncopation between what's going on all confirms for me the concept of intelligent design and that there is a power that is, let's just say, responsible for it all. And despite all the chaos there is in the world, just think of all the things that are happening harmoniously in the microscopic world and in the visible worlds – just think what would happen if there was chaos everywhere. If there wasn't some kind of coordination and syncopation that went on with all that exists. Just think about the time when all that we knew and believed was that which we saw – prior to microscopes and exploring outer space – and how disillusioned we were to think that was the sum total of what there was to know or see or feel or experience.

Raymond's partner, Martha, is very aware of the depth of Raymond's faith.

He is so grounded in his faith, and that's something that we don't share at all. I think it's hard for him on one level. It was certainly hard for a long time because he'd ask me if I believed in God. But his belief and faith run very, very deep, and it guides him. It's absolutely his center. It's shaped by his mother's faith and his own rendition of what he'd like to take from that. He knows the bible front and back. He'll quote stuff out of the bible, which I always find remarkable as I've never read it.

Raymond points out that much of this can be traced to his folks.

I was taught by my parents and grandparents that there was a higher order to things and that, at some point, there was a reckoning that was going to come involving the meek and the powerful. It's something you probably need if you're slaves or a burdened people or living in poverty…you need to know that there's some kind of reckoning coming and that things are maybe going to change. I distill it down to something very simple. I believe that human beings are energy. We may change forms, we may die and then be planted, but the spiritual aspect of it remains.

I think we get distracted as human beings, referring to who we are relative to race and sex and color and physical features and mental capabilities, and we dance all around the real essence of it – who we are spiritually – and I refer to that which we can't see with our eyes or whatever.

How many times have we encountered people, and they look shabby or sickly and you formulate an opinion in your mind about what this person must be like and has done or may not have done, and then the person begins to speak? Sometimes the spirit in which someone delivers a speech is more powerful than what you see – the timing and the situation and whatever it speaks to.

I try to break things down to the simplest element, which is easy to understand. How do I feel about people that I meet? It very much depends on how I feel and how they behave – how they treat their kids. How do you treat your wife, the people you work with? How do you respond to chaos? To me, that's a lot more important than how you treat me because in so many respects how you treat me involves the status you have attributed to me.

My biggest challenge is communicating with young people. To know what I have discovered to be true. That there is a spiritual world as well as a physical, or the academic or intellectual world that they have to deal with.

My experience tells me that I am the sum total of the spiritual, the physical and the intellectual. And I've lost a lot of friends over the years, but then I realize that I haven't lost them; they're still here. I just can't communicate with them in the physical or the intellectual, but I can in a spiritual way.

There are some life events that make a man ponder matters spiritual a little more deeply.

I was probably in my forties when my dad died. Died in 1977, just like that. Best man I knew in my life, and I was fucked up by his death – he was everything that a good person should be, whether you're a Christian or not – he was the best of the best. A good person is meant to be hardworking, honest, loyal and faithful – well, that was my dad. He would take the shirt off of his back and give it to you; he literally would.

So, when he died, I asked what's that about? And my dad's gift to me was a clear and well-stated illustration of what a good person is, what's important in a great person. I compare anybody that I meet with my dad. He was the coolest guy in the world. And my mother was awesome, educated and forever trying to learn more, but my dad was like my granddad, and nobody can ever take that from me. You can beat me over the head with a pole, but I know who I am because of that. I'm Ivy Chester's son, and I'm John Wesley Chester's grandson, and I know who I am and if I try to emulate who they were to me, then I'm ok. If I can communicate those basics, then you're ok. All the other stuff, the accolades, are there, but if they know who you are and where you come from, you're happy as hell. Never in my life have I had a fear of being under-accomplished, of not being able to rise.

CONCLUSION:

LOOKING BACK

Now in his mid-seventies, Raymond can survey a successful life and a hard-playing, trophy-gathering career. He has a Super Bowl ring to slide onto his finger with pride and a room full of prizes in his home set in the redwoods of the Oakland Hills. The latter are displayed in a room where, depending on the time of day, the sun burnishes the cups and shines on the match balls. He can also look back on a life well lived.

He is best known, of course, as a Raider and, according to some, the best tight end the team ever had. I've met lots of people who agree with that suggestion, often lifelong fans who glad-hand him as he walks down the street or takes his car into the dealers for a service, or when they come up to him as he's just mooching around town. Not that he does a lot of mooching. He's still a man with purpose in his days, just as there is in his step. It's always a pleasure walking alongside him, hoping that some of that respect and affection might rub off.

He's seen plenty of changes in the game, both in his playing career and in the years thereafter. Pondering the principal difference between then and now in terms of football, between the Raiders then and the Raiders now, Raymond most commonly invokes the word 'focus'.

> Right now, the predominant area of focus for players is on themselves. On me, look what I did. See me! See me dance! See me score! See me do something crazy. Go stamp on the other team's logo. There was an incident at the Raiders versus Kansas City where the whole team went out and did a dance on Kansas City's logo. That's desecration, you know. Kansas City came out and they kicked the shit out of them. They beat them like they had stolen something. They put forty-one points over them; they beat them like a drum. And for the coach to allow that to happen…
>
> When I went to the Raiders they were not like that, doing the sort of shit you see nowadays. And then, after the game, we partied like hell. We drank and partied and had a good time.

Some individual Raiders partied very hard, such as Ken Stabler, who had a reputation as a hell-raiser and a half. One of Stabler's friends once read him a quote by Jack London: 'I would rather be a meteor, every atom of me in magnificent glow, than a sleepy and permanent planet. The proper function of man is to live, not to exist. I shall not waste my days in trying to prolong them.'[70]

When this human firecracker of a man was asked what that meant to him, his answer was unpoetically succinct.

'Throw deep,'[71] he said.

Yet despite the obvious flamboyance of players such as Stabler, Raymond reckons there wasn't a cult of the personality, a star system among the team. Team-playing outranked individual celebrity.

'I never read an article when I was playing that said "Ken Stabler and the Raiders" or "George Blanda and the Raiders". It was just the Raiders.'

Raymond recollects one occasion when they travelled to Colorado to play against Denver. At one stage in the game, the Raiders were in the lead, which incensed the Denver coach John Ralston to the point that he was yelling at his team from the sideline not to let these 'hoodlums' from Oakland come there and beat them. Despite his anger and admonishments, Oakland did just that, by playing the Raider way. Raymond reaches for that word focus again:

> We focussed on not making mistakes. We focussed on doing our jobs, focussed on not letting our teammates down, but the focus now is on me, because I scored the winning touchdown. I think when you're so busy being focussed on yourself, on your own accomplishments or whatever, I think it takes away the focus that you need on the game, the team collectively, the goal of the team. I think you can easily see the negative impact that it can have on a team, to how it reacts to different situations on the field. It takes you away from the sort of focus you need to exhibit over the duration of a game and indeed throughout the season.
>
> Another thing is knowing a little bit about a lot of things, from ballet to karate. You have to lock in and concentrate and know the role the mind plays when it comes to success in sport, in accomplishing physical feats.

One of the books which chronicles the heyday of the Raiders is called *Cheating is Encouraged*.[72] Raymond considers what that title implies to be an absolute insult:

> Some of our good players have used that tag. I don't know why or where it came from. It flies in the face of sport.
>
> Let me tell you a story. So John Madden did something years and years ago, and I think we were the first team to do it. We were playing a game and we had a slight lead. We had the ball and we were ahead by less than a field three points. We were forced to play out of our own end zone with the clock showing just a minute left of play, or even less than a minute. So if we punted the ball out of our own end zone, we risked having it blocked; we risked them

getting the ball and having it run back and them having time for a play or two, given it takes five, six seconds to run a play and then getting the ball within field goal range, kicking the field goal and then beating us.

So Madden told our punter, 'I want you, from when they snap the ball to you, to catch the ball and just run around in the end zone. Don't kick it. When they get close to you, like they're going to tackle you, I want you to step backward over the boundary line, out of bounds.' So he did that; he caught the ball, ran round and round, and then, just when they were getting ready to tackle him, he stepped out of bounds, over the back of the end zone. Well, when you step out there, it is a safety, which is an automatic two points for the other team. In exchange for being able to run the clock down for nothing, Madden strategized and said, 'We'll give them the two points but win the game by one point and run the clock out at the same time.' So we had to kick off to them again because it was a safety, when the team that scores is entitled to get the ball back again. But there was a chance that they could beat us, so we won by one point. It was playing within the rules.

Raymond is adamant that he can never remember someone asking him to cheat in order to win a game. 'Never. Be in better shape, run faster, hit harder, hit longer, we did all kinds of things to win. But I never heard a coach say let's go break so-and-so's leg. We would study the other team, looking for a weakness, and we might keep pounding someone until he quit, but that's the game.'

Having worked for and been inspired by so many good coaches, it's logical to ask whether Raymond ever considered becoming one himself. He will tell you that, in a sense, he has been a coach all of his adult life but he's never wanted to be an official football coach. He preferred business – like running Lake Chabot golf course. But after Raymond had finished playing, when he was associating with other teammates, coaches and players, he was often told he had been and was a coach. 'If you want to be a good teacher, how can you ask people to do things you haven't done yourself? You have to put the work in,' as he says.

Younger players always gravitated to him; they always wanted to work out with Raymond. People he had played with in the Raiders, Colts and Invaders appreciated the way he enthusiastically practised, diligently studied and played wholeheartedly, his application to the requirements and demands of the game. Playing together, thinking of others. Some of that instinct ran deep, and some of it probably derived from being a part of a large family, having younger siblings he wanted to educate and protect, and having parents that he loved, 'super parents' as Raymond describes them, people he wanted to please as much as he possibly could.

There was also that fearless, no-holds-barred drive to win, compounded by an equally deep desire not to lose, which harks back to a humiliating loss in a wrestling bout when he was a young man, when he felt that he let both the team and himself down. It was a time when he decided that losing wasn't for him, and he set out to win at every possible opportunity. It gave him a fixed goal which could make up a personal mantra: Win. Win. Win. It was a mantra he shared with the team, knowing he always had his part to play in any success or victory.

I love to win, and I learned at an early age that whether I won or not was largely dependent on me. When I look back at my career, I can see that a lot of it was team stuff, but when I was younger, much of it was individual, things such as track events and throwing the discus. Or being a wrestler. When you're on the mat, the only one out there is you. You are responsible for what you do or don't do. So I think that's helped me.

And I always wanted to represent my family: my dad and my mom in the best possible way, then my siblings and then my teammates. I never wanted to be an embarrassment to my family, to feel uncomfortable, awkward and ashamed of letting people down.

That psychology was to prove pivotal during the last years, towards the end of his career, and was to prove to be a big catalyst in his eventual decision to quit. Raymond refused to be out there if he wasn't able to compete at the top level. So he had it in mind that he was never going to be the sort of player who stayed on past his ability to perform. He had seen such sportsmen, stubbornly holding on when their best days were firmly behind them. Knowing when to retire is a required part of a player's wisdom about the game.

Raymond contends, 'Many would say that I quit the game prematurely. I clearly could have played five more years, but I didn't think that I could maintain the standard that I had set for myself as a player. So I wanted to get out on top, with self-respect and dignity intact. And I did.'

He showed individual prowess right throughout his playing career, shining at the beginning and at the end. His achievements make for an impressive catalogue.

> The first year I played in the NFL, I made Rookie of the Year. The last year I played professional football, with the Oakland Invaders, I made Man of the Year. And I made the All-Star team in my first year as a professional player, and I made the All-Star team in my last year as a professional player.

When Raymond sifts through his collection of photographs, there is one thing that very much stands out for him.

> It's pretty obvious when you look at pictures and photos from that time. It was multiracial. I'd grown up in a segregated city.
>
> That integration is one of the things I loved most about Oakland and, indeed, California when I moved here: the diversity. People talk about integration; well, you can look at it that way, but I look at it and think, man, diversity! Different opinions, different styles, different ways of getting things done and so diverse ways of accomplishing

something good, and it's voluntary – we're here because we have mutual interests and mutual goals, and we can work together to accomplish things and even compete to get things accomplished. Integration is mixing.

Taking the knee has become a controversial subject in football. Ever since American footballer Colin Kaepernick took the knee during the national anthem before a match in 2016, saying he could not stand to show pride in the flag of a country that oppressed Black people, it has become a significant action. Right-wing politicians from President Donald Trump to UK Home Secretary Priti Patel have condemned it as a political stunt, suggesting it shows support for the Black Lives Matter movement, which was galvanised when a white police officer murdered George Floyd, an unarmed African-American man. Donald Trump suggested that any player who took the knee should be summarily sacked: 'Wouldn't you love to see one of these NFL owners, when somebody disrespects our flag, to say, "Get that son of a bitch off the field right now. Out! He's fired. He's fired!"'[73]

On the other hand, some of those who take the knee see it as an anti-racist stance, taking its place alongside similar actions, such as basketball star Mahmoud Abdul-Rauf refusing to stand for the US national anthem in 1996 or LeBron James and other basketball players wearing T-shirts brandished with the slogan 'I can't breathe'. These words tragically echoed the final words of Eric Garner, who died after being restrained by New York police officers. While sport is most often apolitical, it is nevertheless a part of society, just as much as politics, and sometimes the two necessarily interplay.

Raymond says of taking the knee:

> I totally understand it, and it has nothing to do with being disrespectful to the flag or the country or 'The Star-Spangled Banner', not even in the least sense. The whole time I've ever played sport – football, baseball or basketball but especially football – you can't find a more patriotic group of guys than the guys on the football field, on a

pro football team, being ready to defend your country or for all the great things for which it stands. I've seen guys before a football game with tears running down their faces when the Banner is played, so the whole idea that taking the knee is disrespectful is bullshit. For the likes of the former president to suggest that is total bullshit. These are guys that would leave that field tomorrow and go put on uniforms and get on the front line and fight.

Just as integration happened in fits and starts, the effect of Black Lives Matter has changed things significantly, as Raymond attests:

I'm a Black man with Black children, and I've experienced so much of the bullshit that comes from the direction of Black being lesser than, you know, but all lives matter, all spirits matter. If I have to explain to you that what we witnessed with respect to George Floyd was intolerable and hideous, wrong and horrendous, then there's a problem with you. I'm wasting my time.

A report by the Brookings Institute suggested the Black Lives Matter movement had been highly effective as it aimed to shed light on police brutality.[74] Similarly, a 2017 Pew study[75] found that 54 per cent of white people viewed officer-involved shootings involving Black people to be signs of a broader problem. The Brookings Institute considered the fact that over 50 per cent of white people thought that policing had racial issues was a huge achievement and, furthermore, this 'attitudinal shift created a policy window for local, state, and federal changes to policing and the criminal justice system'.[76]

For Raymond, BLM turned the limelight of attention onto a subject that needed it and scrutinised injustices that were too often overlooked.

In my opinion, this happened for a reason. It shone a spotlight, and what it says and what it brings to the forefront of a person's mind is the question, is this ok? No, it's not, and if I've got to explain to you what's wrong with that, then you need to explain to yourself what's wrong with you. Because it's very clear and simple. This happens more frequently with white on Black and with socio-economic groups, to poor people as opposed to people with wealth. It's not like we don't know there's injustice that happens. That we don't know that we have not solved the problem of racial injustice in our country or anywhere in the world just shows us how very far we are from accomplishing that, and we have to work on it.

But here's the thing. That kind of injustice and that kind of ill-treatment, it's not just Black on white or white on Black; it's happened all over the world and throughout the history of the world. People have treated people that way from the beginning of time. Think about the history of the world, the history of people who have been empowered and people who have been subjected to the power. It changes. Nobody's been crueler to Blacks than Blacks and whites to whites.

Raymond is clear that racism is far from being something consigned to the past.

Sport at its best, well, there has to be more in order to win than raw athletic ability, raw force and raw power – there has to be some unity; people have to come together. And that's the beauty of people having to come together, culturally and in other ways, to make things work best for everybody. I don't know what the answer is, but I do know that the answer isn't all Black or all white; the answer is a blend or fusion.

If you want to impress me, let me see how you treat other people. Be congenial and friendly and courteous. It doesn't matter what you look like. My dad said to me, 'The best tribute you can pay to me is to be a gentleman.' I want my son to be a gentleman. And there's nothing more in life that I would want my friends, my son to say than I am a gentleman.

A gentleman, most certainly, but what of Raymond's qualities as a player? Is he one of the greats? Does he stand tall on the pantheon of great athletes? Does he deserve his place, as many have suggested, in the game's Hall of Fame?

Fellow Raider Morris Bradshaw has no doubt. He sees Raymond as a great player and a great tight end, pure and simple:

The manner in which greatness is identified today is very different. This is a guy who came in and pretty much changed the way in which offenses play. The traditional offense – four, five interior linemen, center, two guards, two tackles, and then you have a tight end who can go from side to side, and then you have your wide receivers. Raymond could run like a wide receiver, but he played like a tight end. Now you get into the strategy of the game; in the old AFL and early AFC, we played man-to-man a lot. It was still Gillman's offense. What the Raiders managed to do with Raymond was split him out as a tight end, not next to the tackle, but split him out, and this puts pressure on the defense in terms of who's going to cover him. And he was hard to cover. He was a mismatch in every sense of the word. He was big, he was strong, he could run, but he could also block. That was your tight end in those days, and he was very good. You don't become Rookie of the Year for nothing.

Morris gives the same seal of approval to both Raymond and his erstwhile rival for a place on the Raiders team, Dave 'The Ghost' Casper.

One of the things they both brought – they had different skill sets, totally different – but they both blocked very effectively, and they worked with offense linemen and were very smart, making adjustments on the field. The coaches trusted them to make those adjustments because they understood the game.[77]

So what were the principal differences between the two players? Morris is quick to reply. 'Raymond was faster. Ghost was probably bigger, and his mentality was that he was a little more off-center than most people.'

Raymond sees it another way:

> A culture was established in the Raiders where it was ok for him to do it his way and me to do it mine. The thing that made sense, that was important, was at third and eight don't bring me four. How we get eight there might be a slight difference between the way that Mo got it, or Dave or Raymond got it, but in order to have the success we had, we had to work as a team, and then we got eight. Mo might have run fifteen and had to come all the way back to get eight. I would try to blast off the line and get a release and work like heck to get eight. Dave might have done a juke on the line and done something that looked silly. We were allowed to have our own individuality and techniques that we used, to do things within our own skill sets. What people seemed not to get was that we were set on accomplishing the same goal.

Such a goal was realised when playing for a team that grew to be one of the most successful brands in American sport. Former Raider Morris Bradshaw was an integral part in growing that brand and establishing its prominence, not just as a player but when he retired and went into the front office working in branding and sponsorship, building on his complete understanding of the game. He thinks the success of the Raiders brand can be summed up in two words. 'Al Davis':

Al was ridiculed a lot because of his dress. He wore sweatsuits every day. But the world eventually caught up with him and said what great branding. The Raiders often went the other way to many, just to be different. Al generally knew what was going on. The branding, the timing – in the early sixties when the Raiders really did come about, television was very young: the presentation and production of the game. The Raiders were on the West Coast; they got on TV on the East Coast a lot, and, as fate would have it, they ended up playing a lot of close games, and they generally won, often at the last minute, and the so-called Heidi Game was probably the apex of that, in that as far as drawing attention, because everyone thought the game was over and the Raiders had lost.

Television then didn't have the flexibility of today. They had to lose the end of a live televised game to go to this movie, which happened to be *Heidi*. People were really annoyed. Just think if that had happened today. The timing of those events at that time had a lot to do with establishing the brand early on. It's not just the Raiders anymore; it's the whole branding. They saturated the NFL, they saturated the market, so it was inevitable they were going to grow…that's the business of the game.

One of the other aspects of the Raiders that seemed to work then was simply being in Oakland. Raymond's partner, Martha Hill, suggests, 'It's remarkable how the team reflected the mood of Oakland – the underdog, the outlier, blue collar, a little bit on the rough side, the ugly stepsister or cousin of the pretty city, San Francisco, across the Bay.'[78]

The game of football has changed, of course, not least in terms of the financial rewards and the fame that comes with being a prominent player. This is the age of celebrity, after all. Raymond thinks back:

When I was a player, playing football was not a profession; it was a job, a temporary job. If you were lucky, you played for four years. The average was like three and a half years. And if you played beyond that, you were above average, right? So if you were making $25,000 a year and played for three and a half years, well, that might be a start, a down payment on a house, or you paid off the loans on your car. So, if we wanted to make a bit more money, the incentive was there in winning – every time we made the playoffs we did, and if we got to the Super Bowl, well, we got almost double our salaries.

Nowadays these guys are making millions of dollars, and they probably think, 'I'm set.' Invest that. Buy a home. Put some of it away and make some of it work. There's no incentive, no team incentive, no collective incentive for them to win.

This may affect one's mental strength, the determination one crucially needs. It's a game of attrition, and not all of it is based on physical deterioration. So much of it is based on competition. The other guys are champing at the bit; they're on your heels. And you have to perform and stay at a level and stay there and grow or else you don't have a job.

Today the guys are free agents. You have to live up to the contract that you signed, but when that contract is up and you can't come to an agreement about how much money you want to make, you can leave and go play for another team, or at least address another team about the possibility.

One of the other things that has changed over the years is coaching. Techniques are different, as are patterns of play and game formations. Raymond considers poor coaching in the modern game to be part of the problem.

I think great coaching is the essence of the game, when you have great communicators and leaders who are good at assessing the current status of the team and can make adjustments to compensate for any deficiencies in an aspect of the game or when the team is being overwhelmed. A coach should be open-minded and ready to make adjustments in a heartbeat. That's the significance of coaching, being able to make critical changes in real time.

The game has also become much more complex, and not always to football's advantage. Raymond believes:

The game nowadays is over-analyzed – the statistics, the analytics and the projections. You have lots of people talking about the game who don't have a clue about what it takes to make those adjustments in real time to turn a game around – where you're getting the crap beat out of you, and you turn things around to the point where you're using the other team's aggressiveness and turning a losing effort into a winning effort on the part of your team. And the talking heads who are doing the talking, they're doing little more than just regurgitating what the talking points are – in most instances they have no clue what they're talking about.

One person who does have a clue is Mark Ibanez. Watching Raymond over the years, as well as hosting him on his Channel 2 post-match TV programmes, has given him a clear idea of his many strengths, not least as a commentator.

One of the problems in being a commentator and analyst on a post-game show is a figure like Raymond Chester is known as a Raider, silver and black. He bleeds silver and black, but certain games are not going to go well. They didn't go well many times, and so you're on television, speaking to a Raider-oriented audience, and many of them know football, and they're going to know if a player is up there bullshitting and not telling the truth about a game. And so you have to walk a fine line between being honest about what transpired on the football field. Let's just say a game where they played poorly where you can't sugarcoat everything. Raymond was brilliant at maintaining a positive aspect, giving reasons for hope, but at the same time he would not downplay the things that didn't or could not work, pointing out the things that stop you winning games. So what that does is it builds a trust with the audience because they know if they turn on Mark and Raymond after a game, I'm going to get the truth about the game, but they're not going to make it this big sob-fest or display of negativity. They're Raider fans who don't want to see someone rip my team and say everything terrible about them, so give them reason for hope and how they could get better, which would lead them into watching the next game.

We would always try and end positively. It's a very fine and dangerous line because Raymond had built up such a great rapport with Raider fans, and he's a Raider legend, and you don't want to alienate all these fans who loved him in that era, right? So I think he did a great job of walking that fine line, of being professional, knowing how to nuance things and not bludgeoning someone over the head with a sledgehammer about how bad the Raiders are or being a homer to the real fans who don't want to hear a lot of BS like 'Oh we're really good, we're the Raiders' when they've just watched the team lose thirty-eight to nothing. So Raymond was really good at saying this happened which led to defeat; however, if they can just do this, this and this in the weeks coming on, then there is hope, so leave them with something, not wanting to turn off the TV and think their team is terrible, there's no hope and we're crushed. That's in essence why I always wanted him back.

Ibanez considers that:

Raymond has a combination of both the necessary mental and physical attributes, and you could glean that from seeing an interview with him. He didn't blurt out cliché.

There were facts behind everything he would say during an interview, and there was always a little bit of a pause before he'd answer because he wasn't just spitting out the cliché. He'd really make eye contact with you. He would give thought to what you asked, and if he thought you had asked a legitimate question, he would respond in kind, not blow you off as if this guy doesn't know diddly about football. He understands the game, the Xs and Os, the mental aspect of it, but what helped him rise above the herd was the physicality as well. There was that physical presence that could be intimidating if you didn't know him, but once you got to know him, you realized there was a lot more to him than the physicality.

Mark Ibanez has been following football for many years and, being immersed in it as he is, he has come to realise that the dual threat, both physical and mental, posed by a player such as Raymond is somewhat of a rarity. When you then throw in the work ethic that he was known for, Mark avers, that too is a differentiator, a real separator when his teammates revered him in a certain way.

It tells you about how things were in the trenches, and playing tight end in the NFL is as corrosive as it gets – it's not for the faint of heart. If you're not cut out for it, you're going to get separated from the herd quite quickly. It's arguably one of the toughest positions in football, so rising up to be one of the best and one of the toughest is special and says a lot about him. Also, there are tight ends who are known for being great blockers, and they don't mind mixing it up, and it's such a key ingredient in making the offense work, and there are some people who are very good at it, and that's pretty much all they do, and then there are the guys who are good at that and can catch the football and have the agility and the coordination and skill and speed to be considered an offensive weapon, because a lot of tight ends aren't, or even known as, blocking tight ends. So, when you get a guy like George Kittle who, on the 49ers, is known as one of the best or certainly top tier of blocking tight ends, well, he's a threat every time he catches the ball. It's a brutal position.

It's something that fans don't always see, aren't as conscious of, because they basically see someone who catches the ball and runs, but the players, the coaches, the really astute followers of football, know when a guy is in there mixing it up and doing what could be described as the dirty work. Everybody wants to score the touchdown, spike the ball and be the hero, but there are a lot of players who only want that, and they don't want to be unrecognized because nobody really pays attention to that nitty-gritty, nuts-and-bolts blocking unless you're really into the game, watching it later to see how such and such a play manifests itself and seeing what really went into opening up a play. Many times, it's great to have that guy who's so fast and gets the ball, but then you see a little block right here which teammates know and coaches know, and that builds its own story of respect and trust to run plays in his direction. How many times in the past have you seen tight ends that want to catch the pass but don't want to get their noses dirty?

That's what really set Raymond apart, plus he was played on a team, predominantly the Raiders, that was known for being tough. You might beat the Raiders and win a game, but you weren't going to come out of it without knowing you were in a football game.[79]

Raymond has affected people beyond the game of football, as his partner, Martha, attests:

People run up to us at odd moments when we're in a store or in a restaurant and say 'Mr C, Mr C', and it's some forty-year-old girl or guy. He affected their lives, and they're productive citizens who'd had a unique experience, and he is the person responsible for that. He has a surrogate son, Larry, and he spoke at Larry's wedding and it was so beautiful. Larry's a kid who was under Raymond's tutelage and really turned his life around. He had an opportunity to do everything wrong and tried so hard to do everything right, married a lovely girl. And this is a big wedding and these are people from Old Time Oakland, lots of different walks of life represented in the room, his family and her family. Raymond stood up and gave the most heartfelt speech, what this young man meant to him and how proud he was of him, and Larry is sitting there just streaming with tears. In an environment where you don't hear that sort of language, man to man, his ability to be that honest is really remarkable. He just has that impact.[80]

Raymond's friend Mel Harrison sees Raymond's wisdom as a real strength.

He's wise by experience. He grew up in an area which was segregated, restrictive, but with a level head he was able to move in society beyond football and athletics. I remember at parties he was always respectful. I never saw Raymond out of control. There were people ego-tripping out of control, but I never saw this in Raymond.[81]

Martha also feels protected by him, by the fact that he is in control. At all times.

He's my Rottweiler. He is big and he is defensive, not a defensive character but defending his loved ones. If he was sitting here right now, he would spend the whole time scanning the room behind me to the point where I get frustrated that he doesn't establish direct eye contact with me. He's scouting for danger, always. I think it's a residual from the trauma of his youth, living in a very, very, very tough place, growing up with the crap being beaten out of you until you're bigger than that guy, then you don't get beaten up, so very tough stories about his childhood in Baltimore. Black on Black trouble, not white on Black. Then the other large quality with him is being a team player. He was one of ten kids. He wasn't the first kid, he wasn't the last kid, but he has worked hard throughout his life to not appear to be the biggest, the best, the handsomest, you know, to diminish himself in order for others to feel good around him.

Martha suggests that Raymond is absolutely alpha male.

Anyone will follow him…if he says we're gonna go pick up this train off the tracks and save the baby, they'll go with him, but he also follows the team. He will move with the team. I never see him out here trying to direct people; he's in unison with the ten guys or however many alongside him.

In our relationship he wants to do things in unison, but he's always following me. I'll be walking down the street, and I'm like, let's walk next to each other, but he's stepping behind me.

There's also this team player component to him. If it's his family helping him do something or his grandsons helping him, he loves that team thing. Coming from a big family, I think that's what built it in – that get up and wash dishes and help mom thing, plow the fields and do whatever the heck you do to help.[82]

Team player *and* singular talent, Raymond can look back over a long career studded with success. There were the long touchdowns such as the sixty-seven yards he ran against the Broncos in 1971. The statistics speak eloquently of his gifts. In the years 1972 and 1979, he made eight touchdowns per season, that latter year possibly being the best of his entire career, catching fifty-eight passes for 712 yards, with the catches, touchdowns and yardage all being career highs.

There is also that 1980 AFC Championship Game against the San Diego Chargers when he made a play that some considered the best of his career, a highlight which started with Jim Plunkett throwing a five-yard pass across the middle to runner Kenny King. The football glanced off his outstretched hands to land in Raymond's grasp, a gift pass some five yards up the field from Kenny, then he ran the requisite fifty yards to complete what was a sixty-five-yard touchdown in a game in which Raymond caught five passes for 102 yards. Run. Catch. Complete.

His numbers are consistently impressive. He had 364 receptions for 5.013 yards and forty-eight touchdowns, placing him higher on the all-career ladder than the player he had idolised when growing up, namely John Mackey, who had 331 receptions to his name. As Raymond expresses it: 'When you measure effectiveness, it doesn't matter how fast you are, or how strong you are, or how many passes you catch in one year. What really matters is how well you perform over a given period of time.' In the period of time stretching across the whole span of his long professional career, the gruelling NFL seasons, the travel to away games, the rigours of training camp, there is no doubt that Raymond gave it his all. And then some.

When you set out to write a book, you do not undertake the task lightly. You have to put in the hours, study your subject and feel at all times that the story is fully worth the telling. I hope you have enjoyed Raymond's story and the time in his company.

In my spending time with Raymond, I have learned things that have fully helped me in the writing of *Raider*. To push on through when you're mightily exhausted. To listen to your editor as a player might avail himself of the wisdom of his coach. To see yourself not as a solo runner, trying to break for the line, but as a team player, out to encourage a reader to reach the final sentence, the last touchdown of the fingers on the keyboard. Here we go.

APPENDIX A:

TIMELINE OF A CAREER

RAYMOND CHESTER'S LIFE AND CAREER AT A GLANCE

Raymond Chester was the prototype of the tight ends in the 1970s. He changed and elevated the position to another level. He changed the way the position was played in the past, to the present and for all future tight ends in the new millennium. Raymond parlayed the tight end position from lumbering lineman into a position of grace and speed. He epitomized strength, speed, quickness, athleticism, catching ability and blocking skills that was unmatched in NFL history.

(Danny Jones in *Heroes of Yesteryear*)

1966. Raymond enrols at Morgan State University where he plays football under legendary coach Earl Banks.

1968. Under Banks's leadership he plays for Morgan State versus Grambling at Yankee Stadium in the Bronx. This is a pivotal moment in the game of American football and an early personal highlight for Raymond's playing career.

1970. Raymond is selected as a member of the 1970 College All-Star team.

Also in **1970**, the Raiders select Raymond with the twenty-fourth pick in the first round of the NFL draft out of Morgan State. In his rookie season he contributes to the Raiders' 8-4-2 season and their appearance in the AFC Division Playoffs.[83]

1970-2. Raymond dons the No. 85 shirt for the Oakland Raiders.

1973-7. He plays for the Baltimore Colts as a result of his being traded for All-Pro defensive end Bubba Smith on July 16, 1973. During his five seasons with the Colts, Raymond racks up 2,123 yards receiving, eleven touchdowns, and is a key contributor to the team winning division titles in 1975, 1976 and 1977.

1978. He returns to the Raiders and dons the No. 88 shirt after being traded from the Colts for Mike Siani.

1979. He has his best statistical season in 1979, with 712 reception yards and eight touchdowns.[84] Raymond is awarded the Gorman Award by the Raiders, which originated in 1967 and was renamed the Commitment to Excellence Award in 2002.

1980. Raymond becomes a Super Bowl champion as the Raiders beat the Philadelphia Eagles in Super Bowl XV with a score of 27–10.

1981. Following the announcement that the Raiders are due to move to Los Angeles, Raymond decides to retire from the NFL.

1983. He comes out of retirement to play with the Oakland Invaders in the USFL. The team wins the Pacific Division, and Raymond earns the USFL Man of the Year Award.

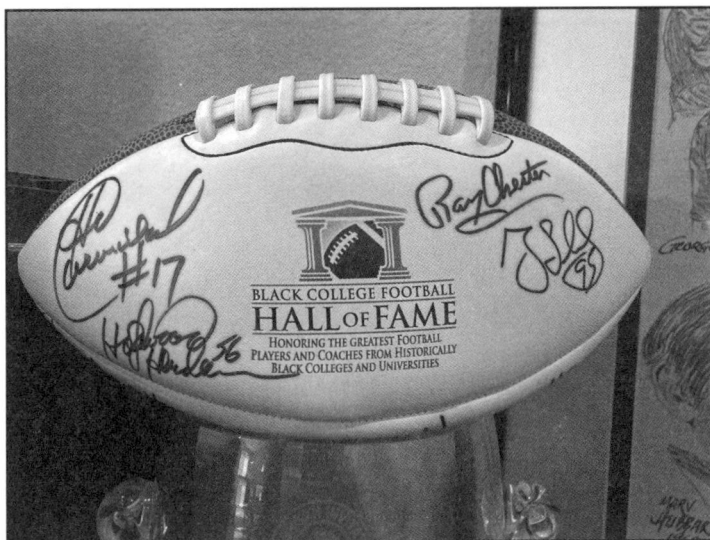

Black College Football Hall of Fame signed ball,
Raymond Chester collection (Photo: Jon Gower)

1987. Raymond starts running Lake Chabot golf course in the Oakland Hills.

2007. Raymond retires from golf administration. Goes fishing. A lot.

2014. A campaign is launched by the Black Sports Legends Foundation to get Chester elected to the Pro Football Hall of Fame.

2018. Raymond is inducted into the Black College Football Hall of Fame. He remains unelected into the Pro Football Hall of Fame.

APPENDIX B:

A BRIEF INTRODUCTION TO NFL FOOTBALL

RULES OF THE GAME

The basics of American football are like many team sports with two teams. In this one, eleven players set out to beat each other by scoring the most points in a game lasting an hour. That hour is divided into four fifteen-minute quarters. It is a game of both offensive and defensive tactics, an end-to-end sort of game.

If you're just starting off, there's a good place to start on the NFL's website, where the rules are explained for the benefit of the rookie spectator: https://operations.nfl.com/learn-the-game/nfl-basics/rookies-guide

While there may be a total of twenty-two players on the field at any one time, a typical American football team is made up of forty-eight players. This makes each team competitive in itself, with each player keen to play and make an impression. Why so many? Well, players usually specialise in a specific position on either offense or defense and are very rarely used elsewhere. Therefore, when possession of the ball changes, the entire team is usually replaced.

It means a lot of men get into uniform before a game.

The objective of the offense is to continuously move the ball down the field and thus score points by reaching the opposition's 'end zone' or, alternatively, scoring a field goal by kicking the ball through the uprights and over the crossbar.

Moving the ball down the field is usually engineered by the team's quarterback. Here is a cornerstone and influential player – equivalent to the scrum half in rugby – who will usually either throw the ball downfield to a receiver or hand the ball off to his running back, who will attempt to carry the ball forwards. The quarterback throws the ball a lot, the leader of the team and a player who determines much of the passage of play.

How far does the ball have to go? The main playing area is 100 yards long, with a ten-yard 'end zone' at either end, in which teams score touchdowns. There is also a set of goalposts at either end, which act as a target for kickers, similar to those used in rugby.

Meanwhile, the objective of the defense is to stop the opposing offense from reaching a scoring position and regaining possession of the ball. A bit like an adult version of 'It's my ball and you're not having it back'.

Some of the terminology can be a bit daunting for a rookie spectator. There are the 'downs' for a start.

The offense, in possession of the ball, has to move the ball by at least ten yards and will have four chances or 'downs' to make the ten yards.

If the offense manages to gain ten yards within those four downs, the count resets, and they are given another four chances to advance another ten yards.

But if the offense fails to move ten yards within four downs by the defense, the ball will be given to the team playing defense, and they will be given an opportunity to score points.

The aim of the game is to get more points than the opposing team, and one of the best ways to rack those up is by scoring a touchdown: when the offense crosses the opposition's goal line by catching or running the ball into the end zone.

A team can also score three points if the offense believes they are close enough to the uprights to employ the specialist kicker, who will attempt to kick the ball through the upright posts and over the crossbar.

Teams can also score an extra point by kicking the ball through the uprights after a touchdown, much like the conversion of a try or a drop goal in the game of rugby.

Another term to add to the vocabulary of NFL football is the 'safety', which is used should the defense succeed in tackling the member of the opposing offense with the ball in their own end zone or when the offense commits a foul inside their own end zone.

And finally, one of the things you'll often hear during a game of NFL is 'time out'. NFL teams receive three timeouts each half. Timeouts can be used strategically to manage the clock or to avoid a penalty or unwelcome formation. Given the value of timeouts during end-of-game scenarios, coaches are generally reluctant to call a timeout until the final minutes of each half. So that's timeout called for this brief guide.

HISTORY OF THE GAME

ORIGINS

The year 1892 was full of notable events in the United States. On the first day of the year, Ellis Island started to process immigrants for the first time, an important opening chapter in the story of the American Dream. General Electric sparked into life as a company. The first public game of basketball was played in the Springfield YMCA in front of a select crowd of two hundred spectators. And in November of that year, William 'Pudge' Heffelfinger was paid the princely sum of $500 to play in a game of football, thus marking what might be considered the 'birth' of professional football. 'Pudge' was followed a week later by coach and player Ben 'Sport' Donnelly, who received $250 to play in the Allegheny Athletic Association Western Pennsylvania Senior Independent Football Conference. Those big-money gestures – and they were a fortune at the time – would become a hallmark of a game that was to grow and grow and grow in popularity, to the point where this sporting and media juggernaut is now widely accepted as 'America's pastime' or the USA's leading spectator sport, with the Super Bowl as its annual climax point. As Ryan Best describes it in FiveThirtyEight:

> Every year, the Super Bowl is by far the biggest cultural
> event in America – or, maybe more accurately, it is the

defining event for American culture. While similar events grapple with fractured media environments and the rise of streaming, millions more Americans still turn on their TVs and sit down on their couch with friends or seven-layer dip (or both) to watch the Super Bowl than any other major sports championship in the country.[85]

The far-from-leisurely pastime of American football, as it's called outside of the United States, evolved from English rugby and soccer (or association football). The main differences between soccer and American football are all about hands and feet, in that the latter allows players to variously touch, throw and carry the ball with their hands, all of which are strictly forbidden in soccer. Meanwhile, NFL differs from the equally combative game of rugby in allowing each side to control the ball in alternating possessions.

BIRTH OF THE NFL

The National Football League (NFL), the major American professional football organisation, was founded in 1920 in Canton, Ohio, under the name the American Professional Football Association. The league in 1920 featured five teams from Ohio. They were the Akron Pros, the Canton Bulldogs, the Cleveland Tigers, the Columbus Panhandlers and the Dayton Triangles, while a quartet of teams were from Illinois (the Chicago Tigers, the Decatur Staleys, the Racine Cardinals and the Rock Island Independents). There were also two from Indiana (Hammond Pros and Muncie Flyers), two from New York (Buffalo All-Americans and Rochester Jeffersons) and the Detroit Heralds from Michigan. These teams have disappeared over the years so that of these original franchises, only two remain: the Cardinals left Chicago for St Louis after the 1959 season and relocated to Arizona in 1988; the Decatur Staleys moved to Chicago in 1921 and a year later changed their name to the Bears. The NFL's present name was adopted in 1922.

Ten years later, the game began to coalesce and grow. The year 1932 changed the NFL and the way championships were awarded.

At the time, the champion would be the team with the highest winning percentage, but the Chicago Bears and Portsmouth Spartans finished the season tied for first place. With no additional tiebreakers available, the league reversed a long-time rule against playoff games and held the first NFL Championship Game. The Bears won 9–0.

With a playoff game leading to a successful ending to the season, the league overhauled its system in 1933, separating itself from both its past and from college football. The map of the game changed, too, as teams in the league were duly divided into divisions, namely the Eastern Division and Western Division. This now-familiar format proved to be a real success, and the division winners (New York Giants and Chicago Bears) met in the Championship Game, which the Bears won 23–21.

This new structure proved to be a great new platform for the sport's popularity, and with playoff runs to follow, fans caught on very quickly and with wildfire enthusiasm. The constituent teams began to change as well. Some teams from the 1920s and 1930s disappeared from the NFL entirely, while others appeared to take their place, with new names from the East Coast and the Midwest joining in what was by now a burgeoning competition and league. The teams who played each other in the NFL Championship Games in the 1930s and 1940s look familiar to the fans of today, as they are ones that are embedded fully in the game and in its history, so not only the Bears and Giants but also teams such as Wisconsin's Green Bay Packers, the Philadelphia Eagles and the Washington Redskins.

A RIVAL LEAGUE, THE EMERGENCE OF A MERGER AND THE BIRTH OF THE SUPER BOWL

There was competition within the parameters of the sport of football as well as without. The NFL started to face competition from rival leagues. In the 1950s, after a failed attempt to acquire an NFL team and move them to Dallas, oil magnate Lamar Hunt concocted plans to create a rival football league. As the NFL Hall of Fame website puts it:

Lamar quickly approached other people who might be interested in owning franchises in a new league, and within seven months, the American Football League was born. The new league was the subject of many a joke in the early days of its existence, but its eventual David-and-Goliath-like success in its costly survival battle with the established NFL did more to permanently change the pro football scene than any other event in a half-century of organized pro football activity.[86]

The first official meeting between Hunt and other owners (there had been others, of course, conducted in secret) took place in August 1959. Things moved swiftly, and by November the AFL had its first draft and was set to move up a gear. By 1960, the fledgling league had signed a television contract on behalf of its eight constituent teams: the Boston Patriots, the Buffalo Bills, the Dallas Texans, the Denver Broncos, the Houston Oilers, the Los Angeles Chargers, the New York Titans and the Oakland Raiders.

In its initial years, the success of the AFL was reasonable enough but not outstanding. As a consequence, it didn't worry or pose too much of a challenge to the NFL's dominance. A turning point came in 1964 when the upstart league managed to sign a lucrative new TV contract with NBC, thus securing more money for the AFL's coffers and allowing its teams to dig into deep pockets to find sufficient funds to bid competitively against the NFL for quality players.

This was an incredible financial boost and allowed the AFL to soar in popularity. There was, therefore, a lot of significant action off the pitch and behind the scenes as the leagues took their chequebooks into battle in bidding wars, one trying to outbid the other for draft picks and employing the necessary and sometimes subversive tactics to allow them to poach players from opposing leagues. It was successful enough on the AFL's side to persuade Dallas Cowboys owner Tex Schramm to approach Lamar Hunt and suggest a potential merger.

An under-the-radar series of clandestine meetings finessed details of the merger, leading to the June 1966 announcement of the AFL–NFL merger. The combined leagues therefore featured a total of twenty-four teams (including newly formed NFL expansion teams the Atlanta Falcons and the Miami Dolphins), and the merger would eventually expand to include twenty-six teams by 1968, with the inclusion of the New Orleans Saints and the Cincinnati Bengals. By 1970, two further teams had joined the fiercely competitive and richly rewarded roster, as the Seattle Seahawks and the Tampa Bay Buccaneers joined the others.

Another pivotal part of the new agreement was that while the AFL and NFL would play separate regular-season schedules up to 1969, at the end of that season the league champions would play an 'AFL–NFL World Championship Game'. This was the first iteration of the Super Bowl.

1970S: RISE IN POPULARITY AND THE FIRST SUPER BOWL-ERA DYNASTIES

The 1970s saw the NFL begin to take shape into the incredible force in sport it is today. There were new teams and new names as well: Seattle and Tampa Bay were added as teams, the Boston Patriots changed their moniker to become the New England Patriots, and the Super Bowl became a much bigger deal, thanks to a few teams growing to become significant and often threatening powerhouses, challenging and sometimes dominating all the other teams in the league and therefore making an appearance in the Super Bowl on more than one occasion.

So when Raymond Chester entered the professional game in 1970, it already had a huge fan base, which was growing overseas as well as domestically in the United States of America and the rest of North America. NFL football was commanding huge TV audiences as well as filling big stadiums with roaring fans. Individual players were getting paid more, and in the evolving age of celebrity, their names were better known, and as many of Raymond's fellow players found out, they could monetise their own names. They could open bars named after them, lend their surnames to a clothing range or help brand some sports-related memorabilia.

As I write this down, one of the largest clothing retailers in the UK, Primark, is selling all manner of Raiders-branded clothing, from joggers through sweatshirts to T-shirts. As their advertising proclaims: 'Members of the Raider Nation rejoice! You can now browse our range of Las Vegas Raiders merch to get your wardrobe Super Bowl ready in no time.' The Raiders aren't just one of the biggest sporting brands in the US: they are a global phenomenon, attracting fans on all four continents. Just start looking around for the silver and black colours and the pirate helmet logo. You will see them simply *everywhere*.

APPENDIX C:

THE RAIDERS: RAYMOND'S RECOLLECTIONS OF HIS FELLOW PLAYERS

In the course of interviewing Raymond for the book, there were many stories of, and insights into, his fellow players that did not fit easily into the main narrative. Some highlights of his memories of key figures are included here.

GEORGE BLANDA (1927–2010)
QUARTERBACK AND PLACEKICKER, OAKLAND RAIDERS, 1967–75

When I got into the league, George Blanda was the oldest guy in the NFL. I was twenty-two years old, and George was forty-three and had been playing forever already. So he was a legend by then. Eighteen, twenty years he had been in the league, been a quarterback, a kicker and of course what sustained his career in the league for such a long time was the fact that he was a placekicker, a field goal kicker who kicked in the old conventional style as opposed to the soccer style that most kickers employ today. George was really instrumental in actually getting me orientated into the NFL; he took a liking to me as well as Daryle Lamonica and some of the coaches and Jim Otto and some of the older guys on the team. I was used to operating in a family, you know, and in a hierarchy, in a pecking order with parents and older siblings. So for me, coming into the NFL as a young player with so many established older players such as Jim Otto, Marv Hubbard, Ben Davidson, Art Shaw and Fred Biletnikoff was easy. My best friend was the quarterback Daryle Lamonica. So it was easy for me to assume that subordinate role because I was born on a team! My family was a team with chores, responsibilities and obligations.

Playing with George Blanda, a genuinely legendary figure: was that intimidating for Raymond?

All these guys – like Ben Davidson, Wayne Hawkins, Bob Brown, Art Shell and Otis Sistrunk – with all of them you had to earn their respect, and the way you did that was by how hard you worked and practiced. Even if you didn't get a chance to play, they were extremely observant of how hard you worked at trying to get the opportunity to play. Coz it wasn't easy to play, to be a starter on this team, when there were great players, ones with history, the names and all that, so you had to earn a spot on the team, and then when you got your chance to play, they expected you to perform. There was very little tolerance for failure.

JIM OTTO (1938-2024)
CENTER, OAKLAND RAIDERS, 1960-74

Jim Otto was de facto the captain of our team. He had a long history with the Raiders, had started with them. He played from 1960 to 1974, so was in many regards the leader of the Raiders. He was the epitome of loyalty, dedication, and was as tough as nails. He was somewhat undersized to be a lineman and be a center and whatever, but he had extreme tolerance for pain and, as you suggest, he was a legendary player, achieving almost every award going, both with the team but also within the NFL. He was Mr Raider, the captain of the Raiders. Many of the pictures you see, he will be in the center of the photograph. He would always have the ball. I have a work of art on the wall at home, produced somewhere around 1973 which shows the All-Star team and its members. I was selected as a rookie, and so Jim, Warren Wells, Willie Brown, Daryle Lamonica, Harry Schuh and halfback Hewritt Dixon are all illustrated, and when I look at that picture, it's sad, man, because the only ones alive today in that picture are Jim Otto and myself.

Jim Otto was a player as tough as it gets. He once tore no fewer than five knee ligaments in one play and was flown to LA for surgery, but he promptly sneaked out of the hospital, flew back to Oakland, drove his VW bug to practice and hobbled onto the field on a leg that was entirely black.

It was as if he didn't have a pain barrier. From 1960 through 1974, Otto played a record 308 consecutive games and finished them all despite not being match-fit for pretty much any of them. As Otto recalled in *The Last Headbangers*, 'I broke fingers and ribs, of course. Played with a broken jaw, kicked-in teeth, pneumonia. Broke my back twice. Broke my nose so many times I stopped counting at twenty.'[87]

When it came to playing well, size wasn't everything, according to Raymond.

Some of the smallest guys were some of the toughest and the most dangerous. Some people think of football as a big, brutal sport with guys crashing into each other. I always thought of it as a big ballet where you had big guys, 300 pounds, running and diving and hitting each other, and they do it over the course of a whole game, and 98 per cent of the time, everybody gets up and dusts themselves off and goes back to their position. So, given the speed, the velocity and the weight and the tenacity with which people play the game, not to mention the stakes, the fact that more people weren't injured, there weren't more breaks and sprains, was amazing. It was a testament to the athleticism and the conditioning and the camaraderie and the respect all the players have for each other. So take a guy like Bob Brown or Art Shell, both easily 300-pounders, and they were athletic and strong, with muscles in their faces; they were just monsters if they wanted to be. If either one of those guys wanted to hit you in such a way as to maim you or to kill you, they could do it. If they wanted to lay you out, they would lay you out, man.

JACK TATUM (1948–2010)
SAFETY, OAKLAND RAIDERS, 1971–9
Raymond maintains that Tatum:

Was among the five best friends I've ever had in my life. Jack was so reliable. The thing I admire most in people is consistency, and there are people in that picture that I know, come hell or high water, I could look around and they'd have my back. Daryle Lamonica was going to be there; there'd be no doubt in my mind, not even the slightest doubt. Marv Hubbard was going to be there. Bilitnikov was going to be there and Jack was that kind of person. Whatever the circumstances, he was going to be there. Whether it was 5–2 or if it was ten against Jack and myself.

JIM PLUNKETT (B.1947)
QUARTERBACK, OAKLAND/LOS ANGELES RAIDERS, 1978-86

Raymond warms to Jim Plunkett as a subject right from the off.

Jim is a very, very dear friend to this day. He and his wife, Jerry, are two of my best friends. He is the epitome of courage, of hard work, among the toughest teammates I've had in my life, a guy I could place complete confidence in, in terms of whether he was going to be there. Regardless of the situation, if I was going to have to go down, he was going to go down with me, and I was going to go down with him. I think he's one of the toughest players I've ever played with, especially at quarterback. I won the Super Bowl with Jim Plunkett, and I knew about his family. Both his parents were blind, so Jim grew up with parents who were disabled. Jim was a great star at Stanford and the most prominent Hispanic-American player in the history of the game. You know, Roman Gabriel was another, and there have been a few others after him, but Jim Plunkett won two Super Bowls. He certainly helped me in my career and threw me a few legendary touchdown passes: he's the top of the pyramid as far as I'm concerned.

TOM FLORES (B.1937)
COACH, OAKLAND/LOS ANGELES RAIDERS, 1979-87

Raymond maintains that Flores was the best coach he ever had.

Even more than John Madden. Perhaps why I'm saying this is because I knew Tom better than I knew John Madden. When I started out, Tom was my position coach; he was not a head coach, so he worked specifically with the receivers and so I got a double or triple dose of him every day, so I got to know him, his demeanor and his style. He reminded me of my dad, straight-going, calm, never got overexcited about something good, never got overexcited about something bad; he was just steady and smart. He had the ability to adjust, and Tom would listen to you and he would value what you had to say about something you were involved in at the time. So, he's the best professional football coach that I've ever had, and, in my opinion, with no disrespect to John Madden, he was the best coach the Raiders ever had.

MICKEY MARVIN (1955–2017)
GUARD, OAKLAND/LOS ANGELES RAIDERS, 1977–87

Mickey Marvin was an offensive guard on our Super Bowl team, someone from a modest home, a hard worker, probably the least well known of our starting linemen. Not very well known, but a really vital part of our offensive line. Mickey Marvin had the misfortune to have to go against guys like the Steelers' defensive tackle Joe Green, 'Mean Joe' Green. Mickey was an unsung guy on our team, and he was steady. He was like a bulldog. He had a strong sense of faith and brotherhood, a belief in God, and, strange as it may seem, given what you hear about the Raiders' reputation, I would say we were a team of strong faith, and people didn't know that. Not only did we have faith in each other, but we had faith in a higher being, God if you will, and it manifested itself in our game in many ways.

MARV HUBBARD (1946–2015)
FULLBACK, OAKLAND RAIDERS, 1969–76

Many of these guys have what we call resurrected careers. Marv was a guy who was a couple of years ahead of me, a running back, and played fullback and halfback for us too. Marv was one of the toughest guys you're going to meet in your life. He went to Syracuse. He was a champion skier from upstate New York, that is, rural New York, and had all the character that you see in many people who come from small towns. He was hard-nosed, loyal to the core and the kind of man you'd want beside you anytime you were getting into something. He was a hard-partying, boisterous, hard-drinking, hard-loving tough sucker and a real special guy.

JOHN MATUSZAK A.K.A. 'THE TOOZ' (1950-89)
DEFENSIVE END, OAKLAND/LOS ANGELES RAIDERS, 1976-82

John came to us having been on other teams. He was a highly drafted player, and there were high expectations of him as a defensive player. Early in his career he had trouble finding the right home. He was known to be a carouser and drinker, and it didn't fit with some of the teams that he started with. But when he came to Oakland, we had so many tough individuals, and what John learned was this… we didn't care what you did off the field, but if it interfered with what you did on the field, then we let you know… you'd be out. So John caught on to that and understood that he wasn't going to be judged by what he did off the field as long as he stayed out of jail and was able to show up for practice and for the games. John fit in really well with our team because we had characters playing for us, and everyone was an individual, but at the same time was a brother, really, and Matuszak found a home with Oakland. He wasn't an anomaly; he was one of the guys.

FRED BILETNIKOFF (B.1943)
WIDE RECEIVER, OAKLAND RAIDERS, 1965-78

Raymond recounts how this Hall of Famer:

Was slight in size, and people said he wasn't super-fast for a wide receiver. Wide receivers are normally very, very fast, but Fred was maybe average speed. But, as his name suggests, he had skills comparable with maybe a Russian ballet dancer or something like that. In truth, Fred approached the game like a ballet dancer. He was so technically perfect in running his routes and knowing how to catch the ball. He had the best hands – we all developed really good hands, Bobby Chandler, myself, Cliff – but Fred was in the highest echelon when it came to being able to catch a football. If it was near, he was going to catch it, and because he didn't have great speed and most of the people defending against him did – as well as greater size – Fred was 185 pounds or 190 – he had to work really, really hard to go against guys like, say Kansas City Chiefs cornerback Emmitt Thomas, who weighed in at 192 pounds. And Fred played a position in which most of the outstanding players in that position were Black guys that could run as fast as a deer, and in many cases were so much larger, so he established himself as a great, great competitor. He set the standard on our team for catching the ball, in any situation, and also the standard for work ethic when it came to being good at your profession. Nobody worked harder than Fred.

GUS OTTO (B.1943)
LINEBACKER, OAKLAND RAIDERS, 1965–72

Raymond's memories are of:

Gus Otto was a linebacker who was there when I first came there as a rookie, and I can remember him taking great pleasure in showing me the ropes, just knocking the heck out of me. When you're a rookie, you go there, get dressed with all of the older players and the first thing they want to know is whether or not you have courage, whether you're tough enough to be there. And then, if you're tough enough and you can withstand the hazing they're going to give you, then you're coachable. They say, we've got a tough kid and we can teach him to play like we want him to play. So Gus Otto was one of that type, one of those guys for me. Dan Conners was the same. A middle linebacker who was like the captain of our defense, just like the quarterback on offense, and back in the early days, he would call all of our defensive sets. You had to earn a spot on the field if you wanted to be accepted there by Dan Conners or Gus Otto.

LYLE ALZADO (1949–92)
DEFENSIVE END, LOS ANGELES RAIDERS, 1982-5

Players often have reason to remember the players they faced off against, and they are not always sweet memories, especially if an individual outpaced or outsmarted you. Raymond remembers how Lyle Alzado was once an arch-enemy of the Raiders.

He played for the Denver Broncos and we hated him. I played against him many times when he was playing for Denver and I was on Oakland's team. I didn't like the fact that he was a tough player; he played defensive end, and many times it was my assignment to block him, block down on him, and he was an extremely good player. He came to the Raiders after I had left and became an integral part of the team. When the Raiders moved to LA, he joined the team there and was a key part of the defense, playing in the 1983 Super Bowl.

TOM KEATING (1943–2012)
DEFENSIVE TACKLE, OAKLAND RAIDERS, 1966-72

Raymond recalls Keating as one of the older players.

He, Ben Davidson, Wayne Hawkins and Gus Otto are guys who go all the way back, probably to the time when the Raiders came to Oakland in the sixties. Keating was a defensive tackle and pretty much a stalwart on the defensive line. He and Ben Davidson loved to party. They drove road motorcycles, and they would go on road trips all the way down to Mexico and raise sand down there. They loved to make wine and drink wine and cook: they were some of the guys who sowed many of the seeds which grew to become the legends told about the early Raiders. They got that going – by being free and wild and motorcycling and carousing and partying. They were great Raiders!

GEORGE BUEHLER (B.1947)
OFFENSIVE LINEMAN, OAKLAND RAIDERS, 1969-78

He played right offensive guard and was kinda unheralded in comparison with Gene Upshaw or Art Shell. He had the misfortune of playing at the same time as Bob Brown, Gene Upshaw, Art Shell and Jim Otto. So now there are four Hall of Famers, and George happens to be the right guard, but he managed to be a starter on all those championship teams. He just happens to be the baby sister, as it were, so you never heard a lot about George Buehler in comparison with these famous others, but he was standard at right guard for a long, long time.

RAY GUY (1949-2022)
PUNTER, OAKLAND/LOS ANGELES RAIDERS, 1973-86

Ray Guy is a Hall of Famer, the best kicker, the best punter in the history of the NFL. He recently went into the Hall of Fame, some three years ago, so he's the first punter…he was a No. 1 draft choice as a punter. Al Davis did that, and then it was unheard of to pick a kicker in the first round of the draft. He picked Ray Guy, who died just recently.

Ray Guy's history made him a Pro Football Hall of Famer, and its website explains how.

He became the first punter ever selected in the first round of a National Football League draft when the Oakland Raiders tapped him as the twenty-third player chosen in 1973. The six-three, 195-pounder from Southern Mississippi spent his entire fourteen-season, 207-game career with the Raiders. His career punting average was an excellent 42.4 yards, and he averaged more than forty yards in thirteen of his fourteen seasons. The only time he fell below the forty-yard average mark came during the strike-shortened (nine games) 1982 season when he averaged 39.1 yards. Only three of his 1,049 punts were blocked, and he ranked second all-time at the time of his retirement by punting 619 straight times without a block in a period from the 1979 season until the end of his career in 1986.

LESTER HAYES, A.K.A. 'THE JUDGE' (B.1955)
CORNERBACK, OAKLAND/LOS ANGELES RAIDERS, 1977-86
Raymond explains that:

Lester Hayes was, next to Willie Brown, one of the most famous defensive backs that we had. Lester made the All-Star team a number of times. He covered all the top receivers on the other team; he was the guy who guarded them. He set records in the NFL for interceptions. One year he had eleven or thirteen interceptions, which is unheard of. That's more than the whole of the rest of the team has in a year. A really popular guy on the team.

PHIL VILLAPIANO (B.1949)
LINEBACKER, OAKLAND RAIDERS, 1971-9
Raymond describes Phil Villapiano as:

> A kind of undersized linebacker who came a couple of years after me but earned a spot on the team. He played on the 1976 Super Bowl team, and he got traded afterward to Buffalo and played there a long time. He was on the Raiders team when it had that ambiance of being rowdy and rough, and Phil was smack bang right in the middle of it. He was an outspoken guy, Italian, and he was noted for being the voice of the Raiders. I'd put him in a category with Hubbard and Matuszak and guys like that – they were real hell-raisers as well as great players and teammates.

DON MANOUKIAN (1934-2014)
GUARD, OAKLAND RAIDERS, 1960
A colourful character of Armenian descent, Don Manoukian played with the Raiders in their inaugural AFL season and is thus:

> One of the original Raiders, who played for them along with Jim Otto in 1960 when they first got their franchise. Undersized, he was barely six feet tall, and he played offensive line: he played guard and was just as tough as a bulldog. He left football for wrestling, which paid more at the time, and spent nine years touring the United States and Japan under the ring name Don the Bruiser.

ART THOMS (B.1946)
DEFENSIVE TACKLE, OAKLAND RAIDERS, 1969-76

> Art Thoms came to the Raiders a year before me. He was the No. 1 draft choice, out of Syracuse University, New York. He was one of the new age of pass rushers, an edge

rusher. He was our guy who played inside; he played tackle as opposed to defensive end, but he was long and lean and strong and quick and elusive. So the Raiders drafted him to be an elusive, inside pass rusher, and he did that for a while and was on the 1976 Super Bowl team. And then what Art did was he became a big part of the community, opened a chain of laundromats and also developed a company that sold Raiders paraphernalia – autographs and pictures and so on. He got really popular because he was at every event and he always had a display of things you could purchase.

BEN DAVIDSON (1940-2012)
DEFENSIVE END, OAKLAND RAIDERS, 1964-71

Ben Davidson, what a great mustache, one of the original guys! He was about six-nine, and he had a very deep, gruff voice. And along with Tom Keating, Marv Hubbard and Wayne Hawkins, he was a motorcycle guy, and they would drive across the country, up to Idaho out of season because you had a clause in your contract that said you can't ride motorcycles during the season. But these were rebels. Ben then went into business here in the Bay Area with bars and restaurants, and he was very popular because he was big and tall with that gravelly voice and that mustache.

CLARENCE DAVIS (B.1949)
RUNNING BACK, OAKLAND RAIDERS, 1971-8

Clarence Davis was a running back, and I shared a birthday with him – June 28 – but he was a year younger than me. He was a good friend, lived in the neighborhood and was part of the 1976 Super Bowl and a well-liked guy. Unfortunately, Clarence developed dementia and he's now living in Ohio. He was truly a great Raider!

REFLECTIONS ON THE RAIDERS AS A TEAM

The Raiders in their heyday had to be one of the best winning sides in America in any sport. There were a few teams that experienced that sort of success, obviously the Yankees; the Kansas City Chiefs had a run, but they did not have the same character. The Raiders had lots, possibly because of the era itself, the sixties through seventies: everything from the hairstyle and the dress, what was going on in California – all of that became a part of the aura I think. And then we had guys who were just multi-talented; some of them went on to become doctors and lawyers, congressmen and business-people.

People both loved and hated the Raiders. Raymond says it reminds him of the Muhammad Ali or Cassius Clay story.

People were excited and thrilled to watch the athleticism and the skills he displayed, but then people hated him because of his predictions about fights, and he was defiant and unique in his style, not bashful at all. He was brash and boisterous. And the Raiders were similar to that. I think people loved the way we played, and they identified with the characters on our team, but they hated the fact that we always won, and they hated us because many times we upset some other, favorite, football teams.

BIBLIOGRAPHY

BOOKS

Burwell, Bryan, *Madden: A Biography*, (Chicago: Triumph Books, 2007).

Cassady, Steve and Joseph Hession, *Raiders: From Oakland to Los Angeles*, (San Francisco: Foghorn Press, 1987).

Chandler, Bob and Norm Chandler Fox, *Violent Sundays*, (New York: Simon & Schuster, 1984).

Cook, Kevin, *The Last Headbangers: NFL Football in the Rowdy, Reckless '70s, the Era That Created Modern Sports*, (New York: W.W. Norton & Company, 2012).

Flores, Tom, with Matt Fulks, *Tales from the Oakland Raiders: A Collection of the Greatest Stories Ever Told*, (Danville: Sports Publishing, 2003).

Freedman, Samuel G., *Breaking the Line: The Season in Black College Football That Transformed the Sport and Changed the Course of Civil Rights*, (New York: Simon & Schuster, 2013).

Freeman, Mike, *Snake: The Legendary Life of Ken Stabler*, (New York: Dey St Books, 2017).

Hurd, Michael, *Black College Football, 1892–1992: One Hundred Years of History, Education, & Pride*, (Atglen: Schiffer, 2000).

Jones, Danny, *Heroes of Yesteryear: Pro Football's Dying Breed of Players from a Bygone Era*, (Bloomington: AuthorHouse, 2017).

Jones, Danny, *Trailblazers and Unsung Heroes*, (Bloomington: AuthorHouse, 2018).

Oriand, Michael, *Brand NFL: Making and Selling America's Favorite Sport*, (Chapel Hill: University of North Carolina Press, 2007).

Rhoden, William C., *Forty Million Dollar Slaves: The Rise, Fall and Redemption of the Black Athlete*, (New York: Three Rivers Press, 2006).

Ribowsky, Mark, *Slick: The Silver & Black Life of Al Davis*, (New York: Macmillan, 1991).

Richmond, Peter, *Badasses: The Legend of Snake, Foo, Dr. Death and John Madden's Oakland Raiders*, (New York: It Books, 2010).

Robinson, Eddie, with Richard Lapchick, *Never Before, Never Again: The Stirring Autobiography of Eddie Robinson, the Winningest Coach in the History of College Football*, (New York: St Martin's Press 1999).

Schulian, John, (ed.) *Football: Great Writing About the National Sport*, (New York: Penguin Random House, 2014).

Shmelter, Richard J., *The Raiders Encyclopedia: All Players, Coaches, Games and More through 2009–2010*, (Jefferson, North Carolina: McFarland & Co, 2011).

Siani, Mike and Kristine Setting Clark, *Cheating is Encouraged: A Hard-Nosed History of the 1970s Raiders*, (New York: Sports Publishing, 2017).

Stabler, Ken and Berry Stainback, *Snake: The Candid Autobiography of Football's Most Outrageous Renegade*, (New York: Doubleday, 1986).

Tatum, Jack with Bill Kushner, *Final Confessions of NFL Assassin Jack Tatum*, (Coal Valley: Quality Sports Publications, 1996).

Travers, Steven, *The Good, the Bad & The Ugly: Oakland Raiders*, (Chicago: Triumph Books, 2008).

NEWSPAPERS & MAGAZINES

Squires, David, 'Chester means business, whether on or off the field', *St Petersburg Times*, May 30, 1983.

Wood, Dan, 'Former Raider Chester gladly accepts USFL challenge', *San Ramon Valley Herald*, January 18, 1983.

ONLINE VIDEO AND AUDIO

Raiders.com, '"I am proud to have worn the shield": Raymond Chester's draft story', April 27, 2023, www.raiders.com/video/ tight-end-raymond-chester-s-draft-story-nfl-1970-morgan-state (Accessed 10.10.24)

Raiders.com, 'Raymond Chester on his draft night and the historical HBCU game at Yankee Stadium', www.raiders.com/audio/ tight-end-raymond-chester-morgan-state-yankee-stadium-1968-draft-story (Accessed 10.10.24)

Raiders.com, 'Raymond Chester Talks Raider Nation', May 28, 2015, www.raiders.com/video/raymond-chester-talks-raider-nation -15342320 (Accessed 10.10.24)

Raiders.com, 'Once a Raider always a Raider', www.raiders.com/audio/ once-a-raider-always-a-raider-raymond-chester (Accessed 10.10.24)

ENDNOTES

1. *Statement on Assassination of Martin Luther King, Jr., Indianapolis, Indiana, April 4, 1968*, John F. Kennedy Presidential Library and Museum *www.jfklibrary.org/learn/about-jfk/the-kennedy-family/robert-f-kennedy/robert-f-kennedy-speeches/statement-on-assassination-of-martin-luther-king-jr-indianapolis-indiana-april-4-1968*

2. All interviews with Raymond Chester, unless otherwise noted, conducted by Jon Gower in California and Cardiff, Wales.

3. Freedman, Samuel G., *Breaking the Line: The Season in Black College Football That Transformed the Sport and Changed the Course of Civil Rights*, New York: Simon & Schuster, 2013

4. *1st & Goal in the Bronx: Grambling vs. Morgan State 1968*, CBS Sports Network documentary

5. *1st & Goal in the Bronx*, CBS

6. Lonnae O'Neal, 'When Morgan State Beat Grambling at Yankee Stadium, More than the Score Was at Stake', Andscape (2018) *www.andscape.com/features/when-morgan-state-beat-grambling-at-yankee-stadium-more-than-the-score-was-at-stake*

7. Rhoden, William C., *Forty Million Dollar Slaves: The Rise, Fall and Redemption of the Black Athlete*, New York: Three Rivers Press, 2006

8. Rhoden, *Forty Million Dollar Slaves*

9. *1st & Goal in the Bronx*, CBS

10. *1st & Goal in the Bronx*, CBS

11. *1st & Goal in the Bronx*, CBS

12. *1st & Goal in the Bronx*, CBS

13. Robinson, Eddie, with Richard Lapchick, *Never Before, Never Again: The Stirring Autobiography of Eddie Robinson, the Winningest Coach in the History of College Football*, New York: St Martin's Press, 1999

14. Interview with the author of this book

15. Hurd, Michael, *Black College Football, 1892–1992: One Hundred Years of History, Education, & Pride*, Atglen: Schiffer Publishing, 2000

16. Lonnae O'Neal, 'When Morgan State Beat Grambling at Yankee Stadium'

17. 'The Rising Tide of Racial Consciousness', Address at the Golden Anniversary Conference of the National Urban League, The Martin Luther King, Jr. Research and Education Institute *www.kinginstitute.stanford.edu/king-papers/documents/ rising-tide-racial-consciousness-address-golden-anniversary-conference*

18. Ronald Bethea, *The Best of Raymond Chester*, YouTube (2014) *www.youtube. com/watch?v=POXhVzLqdE0*

19. Chandler, Bob and Norm Chandler Fox, *Violent Sundays*, New York: Simon & Schuster, 1984

20. Chandler, Bob and Norm Chandler Fox, *Violent Sundays*, New York: Simon & Schuster, 1984

21. Richmond, Peter, *Badasses: The Legend of Snake, Foo, Dr. Death and John Madden's Oakland Raiders*, New York: It Books, 2010

22. Richmond, Peter, *Badasses: The Legend of Snake, Foo, Dr. Death and John Madden's Oakland Raiders*, New York: It Books, 2010

23. Ribowsky, Mark, *Slick: The Silver & Black Life of Al Davis*, New York: Macmillan, 1991

24. Ribowsky, Mark, *Slick: The Silver & Black Life of Al Davis*, New York: Macmillan, 1991

25. Ribowsky, Mark, *Slick: The Silver & Black Life of Al Davis*, New York: Macmillan, 1991

26. Interview with the author of this book

27. Burwell, Bryan, *Madden: A Biography*, Chicago: Triumph Books, 2007

28. Chandler, Bob and Norm Chandler Fox, *Violent Sundays*, New York: Simon & Schuster, 1984

29. Chandler, Bob and Norm Chandler Fox, *Violent Sundays*, New York: Simon & Schuster, 1984

30. Interview with the author of this book

31. Flores, Tom, with Matt Fulks, *Tales from the Oakland Raiders: A Collection of the Greatest Stories Ever Told*, Danville: Sports Publishing, 2003

32. Flores, Tom, with Matt Fulks, *Tales from the Oakland Raiders: A Collection of the Greatest Stories Ever Told*, Danville: Sports Publishing, 2003

33. Flores, Tom, with Matt Fulks, *Tales from the Oakland Raiders: A Collection of the Greatest Stories Ever Told*, Danville: Sports Publishing, 2003

34. Flores, Tom, with Matt Fulks, *Tales from the Oakland Raiders: A Collection of the Greatest Stories Ever Told*, Danville: Sports Publishing, 2003

35. Jones, Danny, *Heroes of Yesteryear: Pro Football's Dying Breed of Players from a Bygone Era*, Bloomington: AuthorHouse, 2017

36. Jones, Danny, *Heroes of Yesteryear: Pro Football's Dying Breed of Players from a Bygone Era*, Bloomington: AuthorHouse, 2017

37. Jones, Danny, *Heroes of Yesteryear: Pro Football's Dying Breed of Players from a Bygone Era*, Bloomington: AuthorHouse, 2017

38. Stabler, Ken and Berry Stainback, *Snake: The Candid Autobiography of Football's Most Outrageous Renegade*, New York: Doubleday, 1986

39. Stabler, Ken and Berry Stainback, *Snake: The Candid Autobiography of Football's Most Outrageous Renegade*, New York: Doubleday, 1986

40. Outside the Sidelines, *Get drunk with Kenny Stabler...Sort Of...* (2011) *www.rollbamaroll.com/2011/3/20/2062734/get-drunk-with-kenny-stabler-sort-of*

41. Thompson, Hunter S., 'Fear and Loathing at the Super Bowl: No Rest for the Wretched', *Rolling Stone*, February 15th, 1973

42. Tatum, Jack with Bill Kushner, *Final Confessions of NFL Assassin Jack Tatum*, Coal Valley: Quality Sports Publications, 1996

43. Interview with the author of this book

44. Kram, Mark, 'No Pain, No Game', The Stacks Reader (1992) *www.thestacksreader.com/no-pain-no-game*

45. Kram, Mark, 'No Pain, No Game', The Stacks Reader (1992) *www.thestacksreader.com/no-pain-no-game*

46. Kram, Mark, 'No Pain, No Game', The Stacks Reader (1992) *www.thestacksreader.com/no-pain-no-game*

47. Chandler, Bob and Norm Chandler Fox, *Violent Sundays*, New York: Simon & Schuster, 1984

48. David Walsh, 'Former Wales Captain Ryan Jones, 41, Stuns Rugby World by Revealing Dementia Diagnosis', Progressive Rugby – A Non-Profit Rugby Union Lobby Group (2022) *www.progressiverugby.com/media/former-wales-captain-ryan-jones-41-stuns-rugby-world-by-revealing-dementia-diagnosis*

49. Chandler, Bob and Norm Chandler Fox, *Violent Sundays*, New York: Simon & Schuster, 1984

50. Rick Reilly, 'A Matter of Life and Sudden Death', Sports Illustrated Vault (1999) *www.vault.si.com/vault/1999/10/25/a-matter-of-life-and-sudden-death-the-1982-playoff-between-the-chargers-and-dolphins-wasnt-just-a-football-game-and-wasnt-a-war-exactly-but-it-did-change-a-few-peoples-lives*

51. *Urban Dictionary: Crunch Tackle*, Urban Dictionary *www.urbandictionary.com/define.php?term=crunch%20tackle* [accessed 25 October 2024]

52. Flores, Tom, with Matt Fulks, *Tales from the Oakland Raiders: A Collection of the Greatest Stories Ever Told*, Danville: Sports Publishing, 2003

53. Flores, Tom, with Matt Fulks, *Tales from the Oakland Raiders: A Collection of the Greatest Stories Ever Told*, Danville: Sports Publishing, 2003

54. Interview with the author of this book

55. Interview with the author of this book

56. Freeman, Mike, *Snake: The Legendary Life of Ken Stabler*, New York: Dey St Books, 2017

57. Ribowsky, Mark, *Slick: The Silver & Black Life of Al Davis*, New York: Macmillan, 1991

58. Chandler, Bob and Norm Chandler Fox, *Violent Sundays*, New York: Simon & Schuster, 1984

59. Interview with the author of this book

60. Chandler, Bob and Norm Chandler Fox, *Violent Sundays*, New York: Simon & Schuster, 1984

61. *Once a Raider always a Raider*, Raiders.com, *www.raiders.com/audio/once-a-raider-always-a-raider-raymond-chester*

62. *Once a Raider always a Raider*, Raiders.com, *www.raiders.com/audio/once-a-raider-always-a-raider-raymond-chester*

63. Chandler, Bob and Norm Chandler Fox, *Violent Sundays*, New York: Simon & Schuster, 1984

64. Chandler, Bob and Norm Chandler Fox, *Violent Sundays*, New York: Simon & Schuster, 1984

65. Adam Kilgore, 'In the NFL, Speed Has Always Mattered. Now It's Everything', *The Washington Post* (2021) *www.washingtonpost.com/sports/2021/09/08/nfl-speed-rules*

66. Adam Teicher, 'Former Rugby Player Louis Rees-Zammit Hopes to Make Chiefs' Roster', ESPN.Com (2024) *www.espn.co.uk/nfl/story/_/id/40592502/former-rugby-player-louis-rees-zammit-hopes-make-chiefs-roster*

67. Simon Peach, 'The Road to American Football – How Does Louis Rees-Zammit Get to the NFL?', *The Independent* (2024) *www.independent.co.uk/sport/football/nfl-ipp-louis-reeszammit-american-christian-wade-b2479543.html*

68. Colin Newboult, '"Rugby Really Prepared Me for This' – Louis Rees-Zammit Set to Find Out Which Sport Really Is 'Harder Hitting"', Planet Rugby (2024) *www.planetrugby.com/news/rugby-really-prepared-me-for-this-louis-rees-zammit-prepares-to-find-out-which-sport-really-is-harder-hitting*

69. Interview with the author of this book

70. Ken Stabler, *Snake Was Being Interviewed by a Reporter. The Reporter Asked If He Might Comment upon Some Words Written by the Noted Author, Jack London*, Facebook, [Status Update] (May 19, 2024) *www.facebook.com/photo.php?fbid=1006278927524437&set=a.592794068872927&type=3*

71. Jeffery Saut 'Throw Deep?!' (2014) *www.advisorperspectives.com/commentaries/2014/05/02/throw-deep*

72. Siani, Mike & Kristine Setting Clark, *Cheating is Encouraged: A Hard-Nosed History of the 1970s Raiders*, New York: Sports Publishing, 2017

73. Quoted in Bryan Armen Graham, 'Donald Trump Blasts NFL Anthem Protesters: "Get That Son of a Bitch off the Field"', *The Guardian* (2017) *www.theguardian.com/sport/2017/sep/22/donald-trump-nfl-national-anthem-protests*

74. Rashawn Ray, '*Black Lives Matter at 10 Years: 8 Ways the Movement Has Been Highly Effective*', Brookings (2022) *www.brookings.edu/articles/black-lives-matter-at-10-years-what-impact-has-it-had-on-policing*

75. Travis Mitchell, '6. Police Views, Public Views', Pew Research Center (2024)

www.pewresearch.org/social-trends/2017/01/11/police-views-public-views

76. Ray, 'Black Lives Matter at 10 Years'

77. Interview with the author of this book

78. Interview with the author of this book

79. Interview with the author of this book

80. Interview with the author of this book

81. Interview with the author of this book

82. Interview with the author of this book

83. 'Raymond Chester' *Las Vegas Raiders*, Las Vegas Raiders *www.raiders.com/history/all-time-roster/bios-c/raymond-chester*

84. 'Raymond Chester', Wikipedia *www.wikipedia.org/wiki/Raymond_Chester* [accessed October 2024]

85. Ryan Best, 'How Massive The NFL Really Is, In 4 Charts', FiveThirtyEight (2023) *www.fivethirtyeight.com/features/how-massive-the-nfl-really-is-in-4-charts* [accessed October 2024]

86. 'Lamar Hunt', Pro Football Hall of Fame, *www.profootballhof.com/players/lamar-hunt*

87. Cook, Kevin, *The Last Headbangers: NFL Football in the Rowdy, Reckless '70s, the Era That Created Modern Sports*, New York: W.W. Norton & Company, 2012